SIMULATION GAMES 2.

PREVIOUSLY CALLED

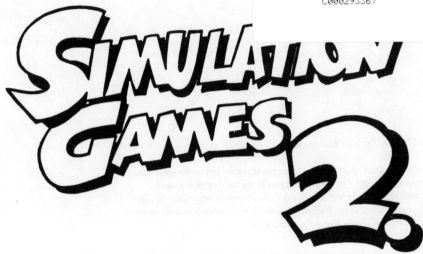

MORE SIMULATION GAMES

by
PAT BAKER
and
MARY-RUTH MARSHALL

THE JOINT BOARD OF CHRISTIAN EDUCATION
MELBOURNE

National Library of Australia
Cataloguing-in-Publication entry

Baker, Patricia, 1932-
    Simulation games 2.

    2nd ed.
    ISBN 0 85819 583 6.

    1. Games in Christian education. 2. Simulation games in education.
    I. Marshall, Mary-Ruth. II. Joint Board of Christian Education of Australia and
    New Zealand. III. Baker, Patricia, 1932-   . More simulation games. IV. Title.
    V. Title: More simulation games.

268'.6

First printed under the title *More Simulation Games*   1977
Reprinted   1982   1984
Second edition, this title,   1986
Reprinted   1988

Cover: Stephen Stanley
Illustration: Michael Lindell
Printer: Brown Prior Anderson Pty. Ltd.

JB/88/1576

Published by The Joint Board of Christian Education
Second Floor, 10 Queen Street, Melbourne 3000
Australia

CONTENTS

INTRODUCTION TO THE SECOND EDITION

Welcome to the second edition of *More Simulation Games,* now known as *Simulation Games 2.* The first edition went through many printings without any revision. It now appears under the new title in a bright new cover. There has been one small deletion in content: a two-page section referring to 'other games' has been removed, as most of the games mentioned are no longer available.

It's rather a good feeling to be able to return to a book nine years after it was first written and to realise that it has not dated. That seems to be the way with simulation games: they deal with things like power and powerlessness, with communication and non-communication, with acceptance and rejection. No matter how much the world changes in terms of political alignments or technology, the dynamics of action and interaction remain fairly constant. Thus a simulation game that was effective in raising awareness of an issue in 1977 can do the same job today.

You may wonder why this edition has a new cover and title. The major reason was foreshadowed at the end of the introduction to the first edition, when we said 'Who knows? Maybe some day there will be a sequel to the sequel!' That time has come. When we thought about a title for the third book of simulation games, we realised that we had painted ourselves into a corner. Where do you go after *Using Simulation Games* and *More Simulation Games?* Still more? Yet more? More again? With titles like that, who would remember which ones they had? As a solution to the problem we decided on a numerical sequence. So we have *Simulation Games 1* and *Simulation Games 2,* with *Simulation Games 3* on the way... and no problem about naming further sequels. To celebrate the new series we commissioned Stephen Stanley to design new covers for all three books.

We hope that you will find this collection of games useful and stimulating. And if you move on from using these games to designing your own, we would be interested to hear about them.

Mary-Ruth has returned to the United States to study, so I must sign this introduction alone. The remainder of the contents remain a collaborative effort — not only by the two of us, but with a great deal of help from many friends.

PAT BAKER
April 1986.

RUNNING A SIMULATION GAME
—some rules for the game director

1 KNOW WHAT YOU'RE ABOUT

It is essential that you be completely "clued up" on the game before you attempt to run it. You must know the purpose, the rules and the possible pitfalls.

Read and re-read the instructions until you know exactly what the game is all about. Don't be content with reading the instructions for the game director. Naturally these will be your main concern but, in order to use the game properly, you need to be thoroughly familiar with all the materials for all the players. Aim first to get an overview — to see how the game "works" in general terms — and then try to assimilate the details. By the time you come to direct the game you should be able to do it without having to refer to the instructions.

There may be things about the game that you don't understand. Work at them until you do. If there seems to be something lacking in the instructions, work out your own answer to the problem.

Work out your time schedule carefully. If you mean to depart from the times recommended in the instructions (or if the instructions give no precise time), draw up your own schedule. Be sure that you allow sufficient time at the conclusion of play for debriefing and evaluation — which, in some games, may take as long as or longer than the game itself.

If you are working with assistants, they should know the game almost as well as you do, or at least be thoroughly versed in every detail which affects them. For example, a timekeeper must know the schedule, a scorer must understand the scoring system.

Try to foresee the points at which conflict may be expected to build up. (Conflict is a necessary part of many games, but there are rare occasions when a game must actually be stopped because the director judges that the conflict has reached a dangerous level.) Try to anticipate also the points at which a game may need a boost by way of some extra input.

List the kinds of questions which it will be important to raise during the evaluation. Usually some are suggested in the game instructions, but there probably will be others which are particularly relevant to the reasons for your use of this game, or to the group which is playing it. Your observation of the game as it is played will suggest others.

2 HAVE EVERYTHING READY BEFORE YOU START

Assemble all the materials you need and have them ready for use. If it is a game that takes a lot of space, know what areas you are going to use and, where necessary, have them marked out and labelled. Have chairs and tables positioned where they are needed. Keep out of sight anything that you do not want the players to see at first, but keep it where you can quickly lay your hands on it when the time comes.

5

3 INTRODUCE THE GAME CLEARLY AND CONCISELY

When the participants are assembled, tell them what they need to know. If there is a written handout for them to read, let them do it in silence. (In most games you probably will want to introduce the game briefly **before** giving anything out.)

Give an opportunity for players to ask questions for clarification of rules, etc., but recognise when a question is better left unanswered. Don't tell more than needs to be told. Sometimes there is a deliberate ambiguity in the rules (when, for example, a particular course of action is not specifically ruled out). Don't make "leading suggestions". For example, in a game which gives the option of working individually or cooperatively you may hope that one of the learnings will be that it is better to work in cooperation. In this case, it would be foolish to suggest that players work cooperatively rather than individually — this is something that they must find out for themselves.

4 STAY IN CONTROL

Once the game gets under way, be firm and authoritative. Administer the rules strictly. Keep to the time schedule. Enforce penalties where they apply. Aim to keep the game flowing. Do not take sides. Unless you have an active role (such as banker or government), be an inpartial and detached observer of the action.

5 THINK ON YOUR FEET

Be ready for emergencies: if something really drastic happens you may need to consider terminating the game. Be ready, also, to feed in extra data if the game seems to need a boost. Occasionally a game takes an unexpected turn when someone tries a course of action that you hadn't foreseen. Be alert to the possibilities of the situation. If there is no actual infringement of the rules you can usually let it go and see what develops. Make a note to discuss it in the evaluation.

6 DEBRIEF AND EVALUATE

What comes after the end of the game is usually the most important part of the whole simulation experience. This is the time when players have the chance to come down to earth and to talk about what effect the game has had on them. Under no circumstances should this step be omitted. (And this includes those rare occasions when a game has been cut short.)

In all simulation games (though in some more than others) there is need for a debriefing period when players disengage themselves from the roles they played during the game. This enables the players to work loose from the emotions which may have gripped them during the game — feelings of hostility, mistrust, dependence, etc., which they have felt toward other players. So long as they still see themselves in their game roles, players are likely to nurse these feelings.

To assist in the debriefing, insist that players remove any identifying symbols which they wore in their roles. Also break up any groupings which were formed, and encourage the players to mix. Encourage them to talk about the feelings they had, but in a detached way (not "I felt Tom really let me down", but "I felt 'Richard' really let 'Daphne' down"). Try to get at reasons behind the feelings.

Once the emotions have been worked out, go on to what happened in the game and why, possible alternative actions and the difference they might have made.

Finally, consider how the game relates to real life: What have players learned about themselves? What have they learned about the situations which the game has simulated? How can they use this learning?

ABOUT THE GAMES IN THIS BOOK

For page references, see page 3.

BEFORE THE DELUGE

About: cooperation versus individual effort
Number of players: 8 to 20
Time needed: up to 1 hour

BLOCKHEAD

About: team work and leadership
Number of players: 9 to 42
Time needed: 1 to 2 hours

BUILDING THE WALL

About: cooperation and individuality
Number of players: any number
Time needed: ½ to 1 hour

COOPERATION

About: cooperation and team work
Number of players: multiples of 4
Time needed: ½ to 1 hour

HANDS UP!

About: team work and communication
Number of players: 12 or more
Time needed: approximately 40 minutes

THE FURNISHING A HOUSE GAME

About: satisfying individual and group needs
Number of players: 10 or more
Time needed: approximately 1½ hours

NEW TOWN

About: role of the church in society
Number of players: about 10
Time needed: approximately 1 hour

THE LIFE AUCTION GAME

About: wealth and values
Number of players: 10 to 20
Time needed: approximately 1 hour
May be used with mixed age groups including children

HAGGLE

About: cooperation, trust and betrayal
Number of players: any number
Time needed: approximately 1 hour

GET INVOLVED

About: involvement in church and community
Number of players: 7 to 19
Time needed: 1 to 2 hours
For youth only

COMMUNITY

About: power structures
Number of players: 20 to 40
Time needed: 3 to 4 hours

SPIEL

About: different points of view
Number of players: 3 to 8
Time needed: ½ to 1 hour

GROUP 5

About: acceptance and rejection
Number of players: 15 or more
Time needed: approximately 1 hour

FACE TO FACE

About: expressing and recognising values, beliefs, feelings
Number of players: multiples of 2, 3 and 4
Time needed: approximately 1 hour

Unless otherwise noted, each of the games listed here is suitable for use with youth and/or adult groups.

EXPRESSING FEELINGS

About: expressing and recognising feelings
Number of players: 4 to 10
Time needed: 30 to 45 minutes
May be used with children, or with mixed age groups including children

PIONEER

About: life styles
Number of players: 5 or more
Time needed: approximately 45 minutes

THE YELLOW SUBMARINE

About: values
Number of players: any number
Time needed: approximately 45 minutes

PARTY

About: sex roles
Number of players: 23 (with variation possible)
Time needed: approximately 1 hour

THE GAME OF LIFE

About: life style and values
Number of players: 6
Time needed: approximately 1 hour
More suitable for youth than for adults

DATE

About: ethical dilemmas related to dating
Number of players: any number
Time needed: 1 to 2 hours
For youth only

C2H5OH (ALCOHOL)

About: ethical dilemmas related to drinking
Number of players: any number
Time needed: 1 to 2 hours
May be played with youth and adults together

YOUTH IN THE CHURCH

About: conflict between youth and adults in the church
Number of players: 6 or more
Time needed: approximately 2 hours
Best used with youth and adults together

THE CITY/COUNTRY GAME

About: understanding hopes and tensions of others
Number of players: up to 8
Time needed: approximately 1 hour

UNEQUAL RESOURCES

About: poverty and plenty
Number of players: up to 80
Time needed: approximately 1 hour
May be used with mixed age groups including children

BREAK DOWN THE WALLS . . .

About: international relationships
Number of players: multiples of 4
Time needed: about 45 minutes

ZINGA

About: attitudes to overseas aid
Number of players: 8 or more
Time needed: 1 to 3 hours

BEFORE THE DELUGE

A game for 8 to 20 players adapted by Pat Baker

Purpose: To give an opportunity for players to choose between cooperation and individual effort while working under pressure of time, and to assess the results.

The situation: The Deluge is coming and, unlike the characters in the Genesis story, everyone believes it. Players have 30 minutes in which to use the resources and materials they are given to build an ark. The possibility of several or all players getting together to build one ark is not specifically mentioned in the players' instructions, but there is no rule against it. The discovery/decision is one that should be made by the players without prompting from the game director. (Note: The Noah story is in Genesis, chapters 6–10.)

You will need:

FOR EACH PLAYER

A paper bag containing

- a copy of the players' instructions
- play money (equal or unequal amounts, as you prefer)
- a tool (such as a tube of glue, a craft knife, scissors, a stapler and staples, a packet of chewing gum, waterproof tape)
- raw material (such as a plastic bottle, a milk carton, half a dozen match boxes, some polythene film).

NOTE: The tools and materials may be varied according to what is available. Some may be more obvious in their usefulness than others. Avoid making any player self-sufficient. (For example, don't give anyone both a plastic bottle and a craft knife.)

FOR THE GROUP

A collection of 10 gram weights. There needs to be one for each player, but they are not issued to the players. Find some stones weighing approximately 10 grams each, or make 10 gram pellets of plasticene.

A ruler or rulers marked in centimetres.

A tub of water.

Procedure:

1. Briefly set the scene and give out the paper bags containing players' instructions, money, tools and raw materials. Ask the players to inspect what they have, but not to reveal it to anyone else at this stage.

2. Ask the players to take out their instruction sheet. Read it aloud and take questions for clarification.

3. Announce the start of the 30-minute building period.

4. At the end of the 30 minutes, call time. Place all the arks in the tub of water. Each ark must carry the appropriate weight. After 5 minutes, check for survivors.

5. Evaluate. Talk about what happened during the game, and how players felt about it. Did they work together or alone? Given another opportunity, would they do the same? Does the game suggest any real-life situations?

Variations:

1. You might have one player without tools or raw materials, but with plenty of money. At the end of the game, talk about how the players felt about that situation. Did having a lot of money help him/her to gain a chance for survival?

2. After the building period has been in progress for five or ten minutes, introduce one or more additional players without tools, raw materials, or money. Let them see if they can find a way of surviving. (This would be a useful way of involving any latecomers in the game. Simply tell them that the Deluge is coming and that people are building arks in which to escape. Suggest that they try to get a berth in someone else's ark.)

PLAYERS' INSTRUCTIONS

You have 30 minutes in which to make an ark before the Deluge comes. This bag contains all your resources for the game. You are NOT allowed to make use of any personal belongings. Everything used in building your ark must come from your resource bag or from the resources of others in the game.

For the purpose of the game, your weight may be reckoned at 10 grams. You need at least 10 square cm living space. Take these figures into account when building your ark. The completed ark must be capable of bearing your weight afloat for 5 minutes.

To get into production you may need to exchange resources and/or services with others. You can:

    use your money in whatever way you choose
    hire your services, in any capacity
    hire or sell your tools
    sell all or part of your raw material
    employ someone else to work for you.

No physical violence is allowed.

BLOCKHEAD

A game by John E. Washburn for 9 to 42 players

From *Ideas Number Ten* (Youth Specialties, 1972). Used by permission.

Editor's note:

The game is based on a children's block game called "Blockhead". You probably will not be able to get this particular game, but other sets of building blocks can be used. For the base, use a flat piece of wood about 12 x 7 cm. You may need several sets of blocks, depending on the number of people playing.

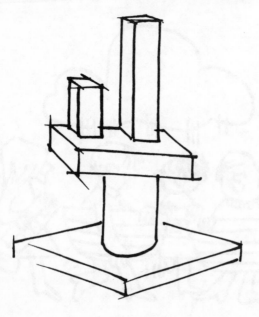

Rules

"Blockhead" is composed of some twenty small wooden blocks of various sizes and shapes. The aim of the game, as produced by the publishers, is to build a precariously balanced pile of these different shaped blocks without causing it to tumble. This is how it is played normally:

1. Dump the blocks on the floor. Players form a circle around the blocks. Use the flat block titled "Blockhead" as a base.

2. First player takes a coloured block and places it on the base. No succeeding block may touch the base.

3. Second player takes another block and places it on top of the first in any manner he chooses.

4. Third player adds a block on the second block, or places it on the first beside the second if he wishes, and so on, each player adding a block to the pile.

5. Each player may use only one hand. He must not touch any block except his own.

6. The player who places the block which causes the pile to tumble is out of the game. The game continues until there is only one winner. The play starts from the beginning each time the pile tumbles.

In a revamped procedure, the game becomes a learning experience. It is played in three phases:

Phase One

Place the players into teams of 3–6 each, with a minimum of three teams and a maximum of seven teams. Play the game as described above, using the same rules. Each team will have one minute to decide who will place what block on the pile. If they cannot decide in this time limit, they forfeit their turn. Each team takes a turn in sequence. Continue the phase until each member of a team has had an opportunity to place a block. Then stop Phase One.

Phase Two

Immediately go into this phase, keeping the teams as they are already formed. Place one block on the base as a starter. Begin with the winning team from Phase One. The play is similar to the last phase, except this time each team has two minutes in which to agree on a rule which they will impose on the next team. These may be rules such as, "Before you place a block on the pile, your team must all do five push-ups", or "One of you must place the small, yellow cylinder block on the pile with your eyes closed, but your team may help you". Stress that any rule is possible during this phase as long as it is an achievable one. The winning team from Phase One starts Phase Two by imposing a rule on the next team. That team accomplishes its task and then has the opportunity to impose a rule on the next team, and so on. When a team is making its decision about the rule they will impose, the decision must be unanimous. If someone disagrees, the team forfeits its turn. Again, the game continues until a team is declared the winner.

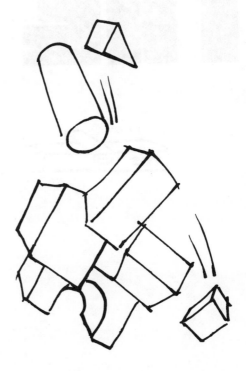

Phase Three

Again, go immediately into this phase. Announce that all teams are abolished, and that this phase is played entirely as individuals. Working cooperatively together everyone has five minutes to build the pile as high as they can. Each person should have a turn in placing blocks on. Announce when the five minutes is up.

Discussion possibilities:

1. Ask the group to compare feelings in each of the three phases. What was happening? How were decisions made? Who provided leadership and how? Was any team out to get another team?

2. What does each phase simulate or model from the real world? Which phase is most like their school classroom, family, community, church?

3. What does each phase say about the nature of humanity? Which phase is most desirable? Which phase is most appropriate for the future? How can we bring it about in our own lives? In society?

BUILDING THE WALL

A game for any number of people, playing in equal teams, by Leigh Wilson

Purpose: To demonstrate the need for all-in cooperation between individuals if a large task is to be accomplished, and to test the cooperative ability of individuals.

Materials:

- Building blocks ("bricks") of equal size — ten for each player.

- Series of questions or statements about people's relations with others.

To play:

- Divide people into several teams of equal numbers (up to 10 in a team).

- Each team has the task of building a section of a wall between two marked points.

- Each round consists of all players answering for themselves a question (or responding to a statement), then placing a brick on the wall. If the answer is "Yes", the brick is laid lengthwise; if "No", it is laid endwise (see diagram). In other words, a negative response means less distance covered in building the wall.

- The game ends when all questions have been answered by all players, the "winning" team being the one which has covered the greatest distance.

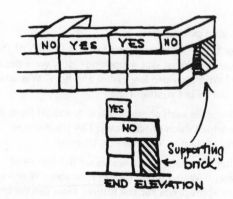

Supporting brick

END ELEVATION

Statements:

(Each player answers for self whether the statement is, more often than not, true of him/her.)

1. I can calmly help someone who is facing a crisis.

2. I try not to give "advice" to others who are in trouble.

3. I don't mind helping people who aren't "my kind".

4. I accept as true what other people tell me.

5. I listen attentively to what other people say.

6. I finish what I say I'll do for someone else.

7. I'm tactful in helping other people.

8. I try to understand the feelings of others.

9. I keep to myself what I'm told in confidence.

10. I'm tolerant towards those with different viewpoints.

Additional statements:

- I am sensitive to the needs of others.

- I am honest and sincere with others.

Variation:

If there are space limits, bricks can be laid in two or more layers. If this is done, a negative answer, necessitating endwise laying of the brick, will need propping up by other bricks. That is, a negative response will "use up" a positive response without any progress being made.

Evaluation: *(for discussion after the game)*

- How did you feel when the need to be absolutely honest clashed with the responsibility to help the team complete its assignment?

- How did you feel when you had to prop up another player's brick, or when you were propped up by another?

- Were there any pressures on you to conform?

- How true of life is
  a) the clash between the individual and the group?
  b) "propping up" anti-social behaviour of someone else?

COOPERATION

A team game for four players by
Herbert R. Kohl

It is possible to play games using teams of two players each in order to get them involved in situations in which collective rather than individualistic thinking wins. I invented a simple race game for four people that illustrates some of these ideas though I think there are many other possibilities that could be tried.

Editors' note:

This game could be played with a large group by dividing into fours. A useful way of doing this would be to rotate the pairs, so that they play three or four games, each game against different opponents. This gives the players the opportunity to develop trust and confidence in their partners. Then change partners.

Possible questions for discussion:

- How long did it take to develop a good working relationship with your partner?
- How did you feel about working together?
- How did you feel about starting again with a new partner?
- What life situations does the game remind you of?

Equipment

The board is a grid of twenty-by-twenty squares (for example, ¼" graph paper). For the sake of simplicity I'll describe the game on a ten-by-ten grid. Each team of two players has a single token. The tokens all start at 0 and the object of the game is to get to the point (10,10) first. The board is filled with barriers so that there is no straight line from start (0) to finish (10,10). Players can take turns placing the barriers or a non-playing observer can place them.

In the version of the board illustrated here there are only two barriers, one extending through the points (4,3), (4,4), and (4,5) and the other through (5,7), (5,8), (5,9), and (6,9) and (7,9).

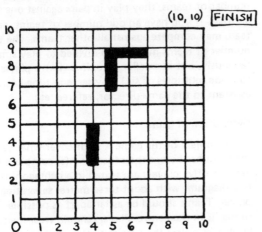

Play

On each move one player decides upon the horizontal move, the other on the vertical. No player can move any more than three squares at a time. The two players on the same team cannot communicate with each other during the game and must write down their moves before either team member discloses his move. They have to figure out from the game situation what is the best strategy to pursue, assuming that the other person playing with them will also be thinking along the same strategic lines. Each move therefore will be determined by two independent decisions which will have to be made with some consideration for each other. For example, looking at a five-by-five section of the board, consider the following first moves of the two teams:

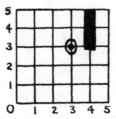 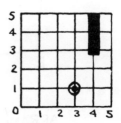

TEAM 1:
player horizontal 3
player vertical 3

TEAM 2:
player horizontal 3
player vertical 1

In the first drawing both players on the team went for distance and ran smack into a barrier. By choosing to move to (3,3) they got trapped. In the second case, the player moving in the vertical dimension, anticipating a long horizontal move, kept the vertical move down in order to get around the barrier. It is precisely this element of deciding both how to get to the goal, and how your ally will figure out the same problem, that makes this game valuable for developing a sense of co-operative functioning.

HANDS UP!

A game developed by Mary-Ruth Marshall
from an idea by Jim Olia

ARRANGEMENT FOR
ROUND 1:

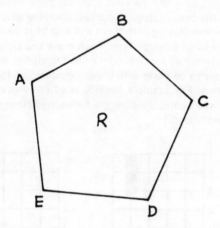

ARRANGEMENT FOR
ROUND 2:

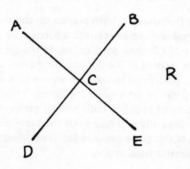

Hands Up! is a game for twelve or more players, plus a game director. Its basic purpose is to highlight the effectiveness of working together to achieve a common task, and to dramatise the results of people feeling unnecessary in a group or uninvolved in its work. The game is played in two rounds, both of which are essential, and requires about 40 minutes to play.

Players

Hands Up! is played in teams of six. Each team is made up of five players and one runner. At least two teams are needed for the game. If you have an even number of teams, they play in pairs against one another. If you have an odd number of teams, each team may compete against all other teams. The total number of teams may be sub-divided to play simul-taneously, but in smaller groupings. Extra players (outside multiples of six) may serve as time-keepers, assistant to the game director, referee, etc.

Description of game

The object of the game is to discover what cards the team has before the other team(s) complete their lists. The five players are seated in a pentagon-shape (see diagram) with about three metres separating each player. Teams should be as far apart as possible. The runner is in the centre. Players should wear identifying letter tags unless they are so well known to one

PLAYER'S LIST:

A.
B.
C.
D.
E.

SAMPLE COMMUNICATION:

To A
I have the Queen of Diamonds.

From B

another that given names may be used.

A deck of ordinary playing cards is shuffled and each player receives a card. The cards are concealed and not shown to anyone else. Information is passed from player to player through a process of note-passing.

Each player has plenty of scrap paper and a pencil. Players communicate only through the runner, and only with players adjacent on either side. (For example, A may communicate with B and E, B may communicate with A and C, etc.). Players remain seated and give their notes to the runner. Messages ready are signalled to the runner by raising a hand. Each note must state who is sending it and from whom, and may only give or ask information concerning one player at a time (see sample). Only one note may be sent at a time.

Every player records the information received on the Player's List (see diagram). Players stand up as soon as their own list is complete, and the cards of the other four players are known. While standing, the player may still give and receive notes. The first team to have all five players standing is the winner, provided all five lists are correct when checked by the game director. This completes Round 1.

Round 2 is played in a similar fashion except that the players are re-arranged into a cross shape (see diagram). In this round, C can communicate with everyone, but A, B, D, and E can only communicate with C.

Materials

Scrap paper (lots of it)
Pencils, one for each player
Player's List — two for each player
Deck of cards (more than one deck if players exceed 50)
Letter tags to identify players (A, B, C, D, E) — one set for each team, pins
Stop watch (for penalty time and to time rounds).

Playing the game

1. Form players into teams of six. Pin letter tags on the players and seat in pentagon shapes with runner in centre. Distribute scrap paper, pencil, Player's Lists.

2. Explain the procedure and purpose of the game: Each player will receive a playing card. The first team in which all players correctly identify all five cards will be the winner. A process of note-passing will be used to find out the correct list of cards.

3. Read aloud the rules and instructions of the game:

a) "Each player will be given a card, which is to be kept concealed at all times and not shown or identified aloud to anyone.

b) All communication will be by notes carried from player to player by the runner.

c) If any player speaks aloud, the team will be penalised 30 seconds. If any one is caught cheating, the team is disqualified and the round ended.

d) Players may communicate only with players adjacent on either side.

e) Players must remain seated. Signal the runner by raising your hands.

f) Each note must state who is sending it and from whom it comes.

g) Each note may contain information concerning only one player at a time. Only one note may be sent at a time.

h) Once a note has been read and/or answered, crumple it up and throw it on the floor at your feet.

i) Keep a record of the information you have received on the Player's List. When you have correctly identified all five cards, stand up. You may still send and receive notes to assist team members not yet finished."

4. Ask if there are any questions. Clarify procedure and rules, if necessary, but do not allow teams to talk or plan strategy.

5. Distribute the cards for Round 1.

6. Play Round 1. When a team has all five players standing up, check their lists and cards to make sure all are correct. If there is an error in any of them, the team forfeits the round. The game director should time the round, counting it completed when one full team is standing.

7. Rearrange the chairs for Round 2.

8. Read aloud this statement of rules for Round 2: "In Round 2, all rules are the same except that C can communicate by note with any other player and all other players can communicate only with C."

9. Distribute the cards for Round 2 and continue as in Round 1.

10. Declare the game completed and announce winners.

Debriefing

Debriefing in this game is best done within the pairs of teams who played against one another or, at most, involving three teams who competed against one another. First discuss such questions as these to allow expression of feeling and to share what happened in the game:

1. Which round was shorter? Why?

2. How did you feel during each of the two rounds? Have each player share feelings. Note especially those of the runners and player C.

3. When did you feel most involved in the game? When most uninvolved?

4. Was any cheating uncovered? Was there any which was not noticed by the game director? How did the silence handicap affect the game?

5. What evidences of team work and collaboration did you see? How did it feel to be a part of the team?

6. Was accuracy sacrificed for speed at any time?

When feelings have had a good airing, remove the letter tags and use questions such as these:

7. What did you learn from this game about working as a team?

8. What did you learn about how it feels to be left out of the action? About being the centre of the action?

9. What did you learn about how people react when under pressure?

10. In what ways might people have experiences in life similar to those in the game? What can be done to make everyone feel a part of a team or group?

THE FURNISHING A HOUSE GAME

The Furnishing a House Game was designed originally by a Dutch Jesuit and adapted for Australian use by Tom Plazier. It has been restructured for this publication by Mary-Ruth Marshall, who also prepared the debriefing and evaluation sections.

Purpose

The purpose of "The Furnishing A House Game" is to create the variety of mixed emotions and feelings which arise when groups attempt to join together or unite. This is done in a "family" simulation; conflict and tension are deliberately introduced when one household is assimilated by the other. Issues such as family relationships, value conflicts, exploitation of persons, materialism, sexual and role stereotyping, rules and authority, and intergenerational relationships are raised. The game requires 45 minutes to play and the debriefing and discussion session needs at least another 30 minutes.

Players

The game is played by ten or more players. Teams or families are made up of five people. Any number of families may play simultaneously but there must be an even number of teams playing. (See the "Alternative Ways of Playing" section for adapting the game for smaller or uneven numbers.)

Materials

- Copies of floor plan, one for each family. (Enlarge and reproduce the floor plan on sheets of paper or cardboard at least 50 x 65 cm. Do not indicate the dimensions; they are for your guidance in drawing the floor plan. All writing except the actual dimensions should appear on the plan.) See next page.

- coloured paper

- pencils, felt-tipped pens

- scissors

- rulers

- copies of instructions for each phase, one for each family

- a set of role cards for each family together with some means of wearing the card (role cards should read GRANDFATHER, GRANDMOTHER, FATHER, MOTHER, DAUGHTER, SON.)

- magazine pictures of furnished rooms or furniture patterns drawn to the scale of 1 cm = 30 cm (optional).

FLOOR PLAN

SCALE:
½ inch = 1 foot
1 cm = 30 cm

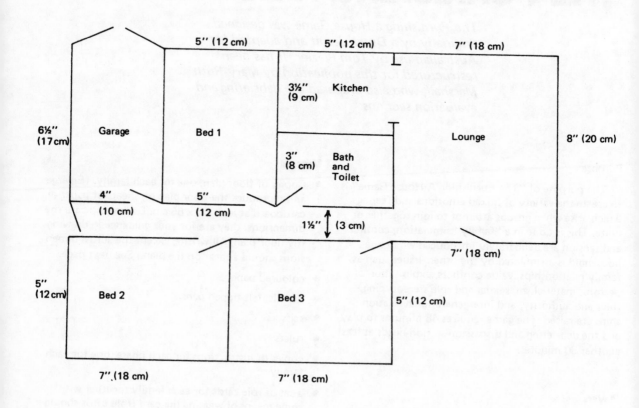

| | 5" (12 cm) | 5" (12 cm) | 7" (18 cm) |

3½" Kitchen
(9 cm)

6½"
(17 cm) — Garage — Bed 1

Lounge — 8" (20 cm)

3" Bath
(8 cm) and
Toilet

4"
(10 cm)   5"
(12 cm)

1½" (3 cm)

7" (18 cm)

5"
(12 cm)   Bed 2   Bed 3   5" (12 cm)

7" (18 cm)   7" (18 cm)

Playing the game

1. Divide the group into an even number of "families", 5 people in each family. Designate half of the families as Family A and the other half as Family B, linking them in pairs of A and B.

2. Give each family a floor plan of their home. Announce that the game is called "Furnishing A House" and that families will have several tasks in three phases.

3. Distribute the following instructions and the role cards to each family for Phase 1:

To Family A

"In this game, you are a family consisting of:

- Grandmother (71 years)
- Father (40 years)
- Mother (38 years)
- Son (16 years)
- Daughter (12 years)

You have 5 minutes to decide who will fill each role. After the decision has been made, please wear the relevant role card."

To Family B

"In this game, you are a family consisting of:

- Grandfather (68 years)
- Father (38 years)
- Mother (36 years)
- Daughter (16 years)
- Son (11 years)

You have 5 minutes to decide who will fill each role. After the decision has been made, please wear the relevant role card."

4. Ask if there are any questions. Start Phase 1. Indicate when there is one minute left.

5. Immediately after the end of Phase 1, distribute the following instructions for Phase 2:

"Your family task in Phase 2 is to furnish your home, **in consultation with all family members.** All the furnishings are to be cut from coloured paper, labelled, and placed on the floor plan in the appropriate rooms. You may have whatever furnishings you like; nothing is built in. The scale is 1 cm = 30 cm. You may choose to have such extras as a car, carpets, major appliances, television, etc. Cut each item out to scale, label it, and place it on the floor plan. The floor plan only serves to indicate the total area available to you and you may change the room allocations. However, you do not have the money to make any extensions. You must have your home ready in 20 minutes."

6. Indicate where the materials for furnishing the home are. Ask if there are any questions. Start Phase 2. Indicate the time every five minutes.

7. Immediately after the end of Phase 2, distribute the following instructions for Phase 3:

To Family A

"For some unexplained reason which is quite acceptable to you, you will have to move from your home and go to live with Family B. You have 15 minutes to move in with all your furniture."

To Family B

"For some unexplained reason which is quite acceptable to you, Family A is moving in to live with you in your home. You have 15 minutes to let them move their furniture into your home. You do not have the money to make extensions or buy a larger home."

8. Go straight into Phase 3 without any further comments. Indicate the time every five minutes.

9. Declare that the game is over when Phase 3 is finished. Ask players to remove their role cards, and to leave the floor plans as they are. Begin the debriefing immediately.

Alternative ways of playing the game

1. Playing with smaller or uneven numbers. If you have less than ten players, make up an even number of teams (e.g., two teams of three if you have six players, etc.) and have each team act on behalf of a family. If your group total is not a multiple of five, you may have fewer (but never more) than five on a team. Another option is to utilise extra people as observers (see below). It should be noted, however, that people become more involved in the game if they have a specific family role to play.

2. Using observers. Assign one observer to each family. Observers should sit outside the family circle and should not talk to members or interfere with the game in any way. Taking notes could be useful. Observers should note in particular:
- What is talked about in the family?
- What does the family do?
- Who takes the initiative?
- Does a sense of "family" develop?
- How does the family deal with the move in Phase 3?

The observers report what they say and heard during the debriefing and evaluation sessions.

Debriefing

(Use these questions about content until players have all had a chance to express their emotions and say how they felt.)

1. What happened in the game in each phase?

2. Did a sense of "family" develop? What helped this? What hindered it?

3. How did Family A feel when forced to move in with Family B? How did Family B feel about their arrival? How did individuals feel about decisions made about/for them?

4. Who took the initiative? How did others feel about this?

5. Who made the important decisions? Was decision-making shared? What decisions were made about

Family A's furnishings in Phase 3? What alternatives were considered?

6. Between which roles was there conflict?

7. How were conflicts solved?

8. Did anyone feel ignored, treated unfairly, or with lack of consideration?

9. How did the two families relate to each other?

Evaluation

(Move onto these questions about what happened — the process — to use the learning from the game for your purpose.)

1. What are the factors which help/hinder the development of a sense of "family", of belonging? How does this relate to our situation?

2. What are the factors which help/hinder decision making?

3. How much does a sense of ownership or possession affect our attitude towards cooperation or union with others?

4. How many different ways was conflict handled? What helped/hindered resolution of conflict?

5. What helped to create openness to the other person's point of view? What kept openness from developing?

6. How can we help people whose lives and habits are to be changed to adjust to and perhaps support the changes?

7. What has the game helped us learn about family relationships? What approaches should be avoided? What approaches are useful and helpful?

8. To what extent did role and sex stereotypes affect the game? How did players feel about their own roles and how others behaved towards them? What ways might we adopt to diminish stereotyping by sex, roles, and family positions?

NEW TOWN

A game for about 10 players, adapted by Pat Baker from "New Town, U.S.A." by John Lehr

Purpose: To explore the purpose and goals of the church.

The situation: A new town is being developed from scratch. Among the first people to move in are a number who have put down the same religious denomination. The developers have asked them to a meeting to consider establishing a church in New Town. Because the development is still in its early stages, the church group has a great deal of freedom in deciding where to locate its facilities — if it decides to put up a church building.

The participants: Participants in the game assume the roles of the people in the church group at the meeting called by the developers. Each person should be given a brief role description. Some role descriptions are given below. Add more if you have more than 10 people in the group.

Playing the game:

1. Briefly outline the situation.

2. Give each person a role description. Ask them to try to be "true" to their roles. Do not provide name tags; the new residents would not be known to one another.

3. Explain that the action will take place at the meeting called by the developers. Set a time limit for the end of the meeting (say, half an hour from the starting time), but allow for an earlier finish if participants decide that their business has been concluded.

4. Assume the role of the developers' representative yourself. Welcome the new residents to the meeting. Remind them of its purpose: to consider establishing a church in New Town. Hand the meeting over to them and retire from the scene. Move to where you can be a passive observer.

5. At the end of the allotted time, or when the participants have decided that they have concluded their business, call time.

6. Discuss what happened. Use questions such as these:

   - what did the meeting decide to do?

   - was everyone happy with the decision?

   - what did the decision suggest about the players' view of the church?

   - did the attitudes you felt you had to assume in your role conflict with your real-life attitudes to the church and its purpose?

   - what things would need to be taken into account in establishing a church in a new town?

The roles:

MR. or MS. BLUE. You are in your thirties. You have just moved into a Housing Commission flat in New Town South. You are a blue-collar worker and proud of it. You are aware that the church is a largely middle-class institution, but maybe the pattern can be changed in New Town.

MR. or MS. RICH. You are in your fifties. You have bought a large house in the exclusive New Town Hill area. You are accustomed to carrying quite a bit of weight in the church because you make a sizeable financial contribution. You have visited many of the great cathedrals of Europe and you greatly admire their architecture. You are willing to pitch in to help build a church you can be proud of.

MR. or MS. SMITH. You are in your twenties and live in New Town West. You're not sure what you're doing at this meeting, as your church connection is purely nominal. You **could** become interested if the New Town church seemed worthwhile.

MR. or MS JONES. You are in your forties and live in New Town West. You spend part of your spare time doing voluntary work to help elderly people. It seems important that the church should be where it can serve the people who need it most.

MR. or MS. QUICK. You are in your late teens or early twenties. You are single and live with your parents on New Town Hill. You are a university student, active in student affairs. You are pretty much of an activist all round and are inclined to be impatient with those who just talk.

MR. or MS. EVANS. You are in your thirties and have just moved to New Town West. You hope that you can really put down your roots there and settle into a community that will be a good place for the kids to grow up in.

MR. or MS. WAITE. You are in your forties and have bought a house in New Town West. You work for a successful firm of business consultants and are used to planning things carefully. It is important to sort out your priorities before diving in to anything.

MR. or MS. PARKS. You are not exactly a new resident as your house was on New Town Hill long before the developers moved in, bought up the land and built expensive houses all round you. You are approaching 70. You are an artist, and your whole life has been dedicated to the pursuit of beauty.

MR. or MS. STRONG. You are about 50 and live in a Housing Commission house in New Town South. You are an invalid pensioner and don't have a car.

MR. or MS. HOOVER. You are in your fifties and live in the best part of New Town West. You are a partner in a successful business. Your success has been achieved by being in the right place at the right time — and in being tough and uncompromising.

NEW TOWN

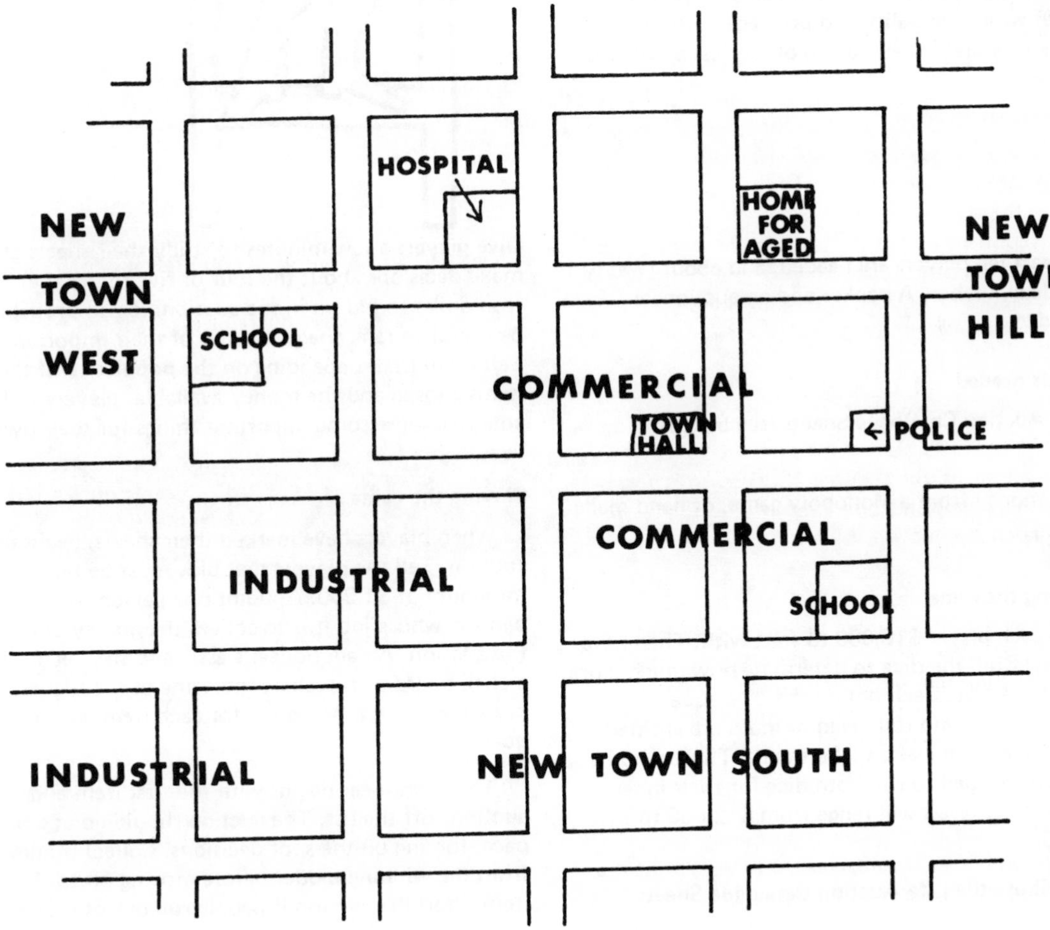

NEW
TOWN
WEST

HOSPITAL

HOME
FOR
AGED

NEW
TOWN
HILL

SCHOOL

COMMERCIAL

TOWN
HALL

← POLICE

INDUSTRIAL

COMMERCIAL

SCHOOL

INDUSTRIAL

NEW TOWN SOUTH

LIFE AUCTION GAME

*A game adapted from several sources by
Mary-Ruth Marshall and Leigh Pope*

This game raises the issues of social class, equality,
and privilege in society. It also allows participants
to determine those things which are important or
valued in life. It requires a leader or someone who is
able to play the role of auctioneer. The game takes
about an hour to play. It can be adapted for use
with families, and has the advantage of exploring
issues of wealth, equality and privilege both in our
own country and in relation to other, less-privileged
countries.

Players

At least ten players are needed, and about twenty
is the ideal number. A banker and an auctioneer
are needed.

Materials needed

- Life Auction Catalogue Sheets (see below)
- dice
- play money from a Monopoly game, or hand made
- pencils

Beginning the game

Give each player $10,000 to start with. Then have
each player roll the dice to determine how much more
money to receive. Each dot on the dice equals
$1,000. Players who roll seven or more are entitled
to roll one extra die as an inheritance. Those who roll
twelve are entitled to roll both dice for their inheritance. Money levels will range from $12,000 to
$34,000.

Distribute the Life Auction Catalogue Sheets.

Give players a few minutes to study their sheets and
make decisions about the four or five things they
would like to bid on in the auction. It will probably
be useful to rank them in order of their importance.
Tell them that, depending on the popularity of the
items chosen and the money available, players will be
able to choose some important things for their own
lives.

Playing the game

When players have marked their sheets, begin the
auction. Tell the players that bids must be raised by a
minimum of $1,000. Appoint one person to be
banker, whose job it is to collect the money during
the auction. An auctioneer's assistant may record on
a chalkboard or flip chart the name of the highest
bidder and the winning bid for each item on the
board.

The auctioneer begins with the first item and
auctions off the list. The auction should go at a brisk
pace, forcing on-the-spot decisions. Collect money
from the winning bidder before moving on to the next
item. Stop the auction if people run out of money.

Discussing the game

1. Who was not able to buy anything? Did anyone have more than one item? Did everyone get their first choice? Did anyone buy an item not in the original choices?

2. How did the wealthy people feel during this game? How did the poor people feel? What was the basis of privilege?

3. Were there any items important to players which were not on the list? Assess the worth of these additional items in comparison to the prices fetched by items on the main list.

4. What are the really important things in life? Are they actually things money can buy? To what degree are the most important things related to privilege or status in society?

5. Look at the items which received the highest bids. Are they aspects of life most members would agree are important?

6. Who was the winner in the game? Or were there several winners?

Ways of adapting the game

If families are playing the game, double the amounts of money, and allow time for the family to discuss the things it wishes to bid for. Or you might make up fictitious names for countries and assign them to players. Instead of money, use a point system (rolling an eight means you have eight points to bid), and have players bid for the values they would like their countries to have. Countries might form a coalition or union, pooling their resources to gain benefit for all. The auctioneer might sometimes add an arbitary $5,000 to the cost of something, blaming "the energy crisis" or "worldwide inflation" or "the brain drain". Finally, you may wish to adapt or add to the Life Auction Catalogue.

LIFE AUCTION CATALOGUE SHEET

1. Artistic ability
2. Power over things (fix cars, program computers, etc.)
3. Vast wealth
4. Physical attractiveness
5. Ability to give love
6. Ability to draw love from others
7. Close and supportive family life
8. Strong and growing faith
9. Ability to initiate and maintain friendships
10. Offspring who are a credit to you
11. Active and satisfying sex life
12. Ability to influence others
13. Power over other people
14. Active and satisfying athletic life
15. Opportunities for risk and adventure
16. Ability to think quickly and logically
17. Good health
18. Popularity with the opposite sex
19. Creativity
20. Musical talent
21. A superior mind
22. Ability to speak well in public
23. Activity which contributes to the good of society
24. Social prestige
25. A happy and warm marriage
26. Ability to bounce back

Haggle

A game by Sid Sackson
for any number of players

The setup for Haggle varies with the number of players, with the preferences of those preparing the game, and also with the necessity of making changes if part, or all, of a group has played before. The following actual game, one that involved fifteen participants, illustrates the equipment required and the general rules of play. You can take it from there.

Reprinted from *A Gamut of Games* by Sidney Sackson (Random House, 1969). Used by permission.

Equipment

● Small blank cards in five different colours. About 8 x 5cm is a good size. Suggested colours: yellow, blue, red, orange and white. (It is not a good idea to use both blue and green since they can be confused.) You will need twice as many of each colour as there are players in the game. (Thus for fifteen players, thirty cards of each colour were prepared.)

● Envelopes, one for each player.

● Secret information sheets. These are slips of paper on which information concerning the values of the coloured cards are typed or printed. One piece of information is required for each player in the game and two slips are prepared for each piece of information. (Thus for fifteen players, thirty secret information sheets were prepared.) The following are the information sheets used in the actual game:

1. Orange cards have a basic value of 4 and are equal to a red card and a yellow card.

2. White cards have the highest basic value and are equal to a red card and a blue card.

3. Blue cards have a basic value twice that of yellow and half that of orange.

4. If a player has more than three white cards, all of his white cards lose their value.

5. A player can score only as many orange cards as he has blue cards.

6. If a player has five or more blue cards, 10 points are deducted from every other player's score.

7. A set of three red cards protects you from one set of five blue cards.

8. The player with the most yellow cards gets a bonus of that number of cards squared. (For example, if most yellow cards are 5, bonus is 25.) If two or more players tie for most yellow, they are eliminated and bonus goes to the next highest.

9. If a player hands in seven or more cards of the same colour, he is eliminated from the game.

10. Each set of five different colours gives a bonus of 10 points.

11. If a "pyramid" is handed in with no other cards, the value of the hand is doubled. A pyramid consists of four cards of one colour, three cards of a second colour, two cards of a third colour, and one card of a fourth colour.

12. The player with the most red cards doubles their value. In case of a tie, no player collects the extra value.

13. Each set of two yellow cards doubles the value of one white card.

14. Each set of three blue cards quadruples the value of one orange card.

15. No more than thirteen cards in a hand can be scored. If more are handed in, the excess will be removed at random.

Preliminary

All of the cards are well shuffled and then dealt into piles of ten cards each. Each pile of cards is placed in an envelope together with two information sheets (chosen at random, except that duplicates should not be placed in the same envelope).

The play

The envelopes are distributed, one to each player, with the following explanation.

The object of the game is to collect the most valuable hand of cards. In order to learn what constitutes a valuable hand you will have to read as many of the information sheets as possible. As you begin to obtain information you will want to get hold of certain cards and, possibly, to get rid of others. You are free to approach any other player at any time with a proposition to trade information or cards, or both. And, of course, it pays to haggle over the terms in an attempt to gain the most and give up the least.

At an appointed time you will place your cards in an envelope, mark it with your name, and hand it in for scoring. If you feel it is to your advantage, it is permissible to omit some of the cards you hold at the end of the game from those submitted as your hand.

Scoring the hands

Each hand is scored taking into consideration all the data supplied on the information sheets.

Using the fifteen pieces of information from the game we have been following, let's look at the scoring of some of the hands. The basic values of the colours (which can be deduced from the first three information sheets) are: yellow = 1, blue = 2, red = 3, orange = 4, and white = 5.

Hand #1 consists of B.B.B.B.B.B.R.O.O.O.W. The six blue cards score 12 points. The red card scores 3 points. Two orange cards score 16 points each (see information sheet 14) and the third scores 4 points. The white card scores 5 points. The total score is 56 points. The blue cards also cause every other player to lose 10 points (see information sheet 6).

Hand #2 consists of Y.Y.Y.B.B.R.R.O.O.O.W.W.W.— thirteen cards, which is the maximum that can be scored (see information sheet 15). The three yellow cards score 3 points. The two blue cards score 4 points. The two red cards score 6 points. Only two of the three orange cards can be scored (see information sheet 5) at 4 points each for a total of 8 points. One white card scores 10 points (see information sheet 13) while the other two score 5 points each for a total of 20 points. There are 20 points in bonuses (see information sheet 10) but there is also a deduction of 10 points for player #1's five blue cards. The final score is 51 points.

Hand #3 consists of B.B.R.R.R.R.R.O.O.W.W. The two blue cards score 4 points. The five red cards are the largest number of this colour in any hand and double their value (see information sheet 12) to a total of 30 points. The red cards also protect against the deduction for player #1's five blue cards (see information sheet 7). The two orange cards score 8. The two white cards score 10. The total score is 52 points.

Hand #4 consists of Y.Y.Y.Y.B.B.R.R.R.W. The four yellow cards score 4 points. The two blue cards score 4 points. The three red cards score 9 points, and protect against a deduction. The one white card scores 10 points (see information sheet 13). This totals to 27 points and since the hand is a pyramid (see information sheet 11) this doubles to 54 points, the final score.

Hand #5 consists of Y.Y.Y.Y.Y.Y.R.W.W. The six yellow cards (one more would have voided the hand — see information sheet 9) score 6 points. The one red card scores 3 points. The two white cards score 20 points. The six yellow cards are the largest number of this colour and earn a bonus of 36 points (see information sheet 8). This adds up to 65 points, but there is a 10-point deduction for the five blue cards, so the final score is 55 points.

A few final remarks

The first thing a player has to do in order to play well is to gain information as quickly as possible. Deals for exchange of information can take many forms. Players can agree to trade sheets, sight unseen, but run the risk of getting information they already have. Or players can tell each other the sheet number before trading. The deal can involve reading another player's sheet without actually gaining possession of it or even being told about the contents of a sheet without seeing it. In the latter case it is possible to obtain misinformation either by accident or by design.

A player should keep track of the sheet numbers he has seen and, unless he has a good memory, it is desirable to make notes about their contents. It is not always possible to obtain all the information nor is it always necessary. A player with a little information and a lot of luck can collect a hand of cards that just happen to fit together well enough to win.

A clever, but dirty, trick is for a player to obtain possession, early in the game, of two information sheets with the same number. He can then drive a hard bargain from those who want to see this information or can simply refuse to let anyone see it.

A player can ask for a card or cards as part of a deal in exchanging information. He can also stipulate, providing of course that the other player agrees, that he can choose the card or cards at a later time.

The above is not meant to cover all the possible forms that trading can take since any deal that two, or more, players agree on can be made. The ultimate, to my knowledge, in hard dealing occurred in one game when a player insisted upon, and received, the prize as payment for helping the other player win it.

Editor's note

The author designed this game as a party game, ending with the scoring and awarding of a prize. We would, however, suggest ending with a discussion along the following lines:

- Who was the winner and why?
- How did you feel about the game, and particularly about the tactics used by other players?
- What tactics did you use? How did you feel about them?
- Did you feel that you could trust others?
- What similarities do you see between the game situation and situations in real-life?

GET INVOLVED

A game for 7 to 19 players by Colin Ray

Purpose

This is a fun program which will help you and your group to discover how involved and concerned you really are for the needs of the church and community.

Preparation

1. You will need a large room such as a club room or church hall, with the floor cleared.

2. Mark twenty squares on the floor at intervals around the room. Draw them with chalk, or fix sheets of quarto paper to the floor with masking tape. Number them in sequence, 1 to 20. Numbers 3, 8, 11, 16 and 19 should be coloured, (these are SURPRISE squares), the others white. (Use coloured chalk or paper for the coloured squares.)

3. The game is played with teams of two or three players, depending on how many people you want to involve. Place two or three chairs beside each square, depending on what size teams you are using.

4. Make a big dice (a cardboard carton covered with paper).

5. Prepare three sets of cards, a different colour for each set. You will need about 20 ODDS, 20 EVENS, and 10 SURPRISE cards. The ODDS have questions about the church and faith, the EVENS questions about citizenship and community, and the SURPRISES special instructions. See below for suggestions, or make up your own questions.

6. Prepare some kind of identification tags for the teams so that they can be called by colour, name, or whatever.

Procedure

1. Determine whether you are going to play as pair teams or triplet teams. Six pairs (12 people) or six triplets (18 people) is the biggest combination suggested to play the game. Choose the teams.

2. In addition you will need an Umpire, who will direct the action of the game, roll the dice, and act as "runner" to take the cards to the teams. The Umpire operates from the centre of the room.

3. Determine (by drawing straws or some other method) the order in which the teams will play.

4. The Umpire throws the dice to begin play. Team No. 1 moves to the appropriate square. (Say a 4 is thrown. The players from team 1 move to square 4, sit down on the chairs provided, and receive an EVENS card from the Umpire. If a 5 had been thrown they would have gone to square 5 and been given an ODDS card. If a 3 came up they would have gone to square 3 and received a SURPRISE card.)

5. If the team has received an ODDS or EVENS card, members have 30 seconds in which to decide whether or not they will answer the question and if so, whether the answer will be given by one member of the team or all. One minute speaking time is allowed for answering.

6. Remember, the name and aim of the game is GET INVOLVED. However, a team may choose to "pass", in which case the question is NOT READ OUT LOUD and the team moves back 2 squares.

7. If the team decides to answer the question, a team member reads it out loud and then it is answered. The other teams listen and then the members of each team quickly confer on whether or not they are satisfied with the answer.

8. The Umpire calls "VOTE". Those teams satisfied with the answer give the THUMBS UP signal. If dissatisfied they vote THUMBS DOWN. If they are undecided, or the members cannot agree, they sit with arms folded. The umpire calculates the score, which is the difference between the number of teams with thumbs up and those with thumbs down. The team whose answer is being assessed moves forward or backward that number of squares. Any team voting "undecided" must move back one square.

9. Any team voting "thumbs down" must now give its reasons for so voting.

10. All answers must be clearly audible. Otherwise a penalty (back one square) may be demanded by the other teams. Any dispute in this regard should be settled by voting.

11. Any team landing on a square already occupied by another team must go back to the nearest vacant chairs. However, they receive the card indicated by the square they landed on, and count their move from that square. For example, if a throw takes a team to square 11, and another team is already there, the new team moves back to the square 10 chairs but, instead of receiving an EVENS card (as the team would if it actually landed on square 10) the team gets a SURPRISE card for square 11. Suppose the SURPRISE is one which involves voting by the other teams, and the result of the vote is a forward move of 2 squares. The team moves forward two squares from square 11, which takes it to square 13.

12. The teams continue to move, in turn, until one team has passed square 20 and is pronounced the winner.

Debriefing (after the game)

Help players to reflect on the game by asking questions such as these:

1. How did you feel as the game progressed?

2. Was there cooperation in your team? Did you feel you were able to help each other? Did one person leave it to the other person(s) all the time? Did one person take over all the time?

3. How honest were you? When another team was getting ahead did you ever "do the dirty" on them and give them a thumbs down? Were you honest in your answers, or did you say what you thought people would like to hear you say?

4. How determined were you to win?

5. What does this game say about life and living?

ODDS CARDS — about the church and faith

1.   What do you think should be the role or task of a minister?

2.   Your youth group is going to be closed down. What can you do about it?

3.   How can relationships between different denominations be improved?

4.   What is the most important thing that the Bible reveals to you?

5.   Can the Bible, written hundreds of years ago, still be relevant for people today?

6.   Name an important social problem in your community. What should the church be doing about it?

7.   What qualities would you expect to find in a Christian leader?

8.   What do you mean when you say worship?

9.   What would you do to "brighten up" your church worship services?

10.   What is the most suitable kind of music for use in worship?

11.   In what ways could your youth group serve the community?

12.   What can a youth group do to help bridge the "generation gap"?

13.   How would you describe a Christian?

14.   What is the most important task for the church today?

15.   What does Christmas mean to you?

16.   What does Easter mean to you?

17.   Do the Ten Commandments have any relevance for today?

18.   What is the best way for a Christian to witness to his/her faith?

19.   What happens when we pray?

20.   Can a person be a Christian without going to church?

EVENS CARDS — about citizenship and community

1.   Should people be free to decide whether or not they wish to work for a living?

2.   What do the Olympic Games achieve?

3.   What is the biggest mistake your country made in the past twelve months?

4.   What's good about being a citizen of your country?

5.   What is a gentleman?

6.   What would you do to encourage tourism in your country?

7.   How can you best help immigrants in your country?

8.   Is the morality of today's society declining?

9.   What is your attitude to public demonstrations?

10. What are some of the qualities of a good leader?

11. What do you think about Women's Lib?

12. If you had the necessary money, what country in the world would you choose to visit, and why?

13. Is your country a nation of spectator sportsmen?

14. Who is the most important person alive in the world today?

15. In what ways can young people be helpful to aged people?

16. What value are trade unions?

17. What is a lady?

18. What is wrong with gambling?

19. Should the use of marijuana be decriminalised?

20. Is censorship necessary?

SURPRISE CARDS

1. Choose a Bible story or proverb. Mime it for the other teams. If any other team can identify your mime, both that team and your team move forward one square.

2. Read this aloud:
Imagine that your team has been asked to nominate a young person (under 30) from your country to attend a world youth conference. Each team must make a nomination, and must have three good reasons for their choice. Teams will take it in turns to state their nomination and their reasons, and we will vote on each team's statement.

3. This is a secret card and may be kept by your team. (That is as much as you should tell the other teams at this stage. One effective way of getting on is to cheat a little. Try moving an extra square each time you advance. If caught, apologise, miss one turn, read the rest of this card to the group, and try honesty for a change of policy!)

4. Sorry, no surprise for you, but you can move forward one square.

5. Use your imagination. One of your team has been blinded. (Decide which one of you it is. That person closes his/her eyes and keeps them closed until further notice.) On your team's next move the blind member must be led by another member until safely seated. At that point his/her sight is restored UNLESS the move lands you on another SURPRISE square, in which case the blind player remains blind for another turn, and you do not receive another SURPRISE card. The blind player must trust his/her partner, and the partner must be completely trust-worthy.

6. Sad surprise! All teams move back to square one.

7. **Do not read this aloud.** You have one minute in which to set everyone else in the room laughing. If you succeed, move forward two spaces. If you fail, move back one space for each team not laughing.

8. **Do not read this aloud.** Quickly decide on a pleasant surprise that you can give right now to some-one else in the room (not a member of your team). Act on your decision. Then ask the other teams to vote on whether or not it was a pleasant surprise. Move forward or back as indicated by their votes.

9. Use your imagination. Within 2 minutes, give your own and every other team a nickname. Forward 1 space for each name.

10. **Do not read this aloud.** You have one minute in which to make a member of another team say "thank you". Forward two squares if you succeed, back one for each unsuccessful attempt.

COMMUNITY

A game for 20—40 people

From *Power Quotient Bag* "Two Power Games" published by AAUW. Used with the permission of the American Association of University Women.

Introduction to Community

"Community" is a game which enables participants to learn more about community power structures and the use of power in the community. It is a partial replica of a community and the power groups which may be found therein. "Community" focuses upon group patterns of power relations and their operation with city government. It may be played by 20—40 people and it will require a minimum of three hours. This time period may be extended and broken up into two-hour units.

Community is designed to:

● Direct peoples' thinking to the potential and problems of community life.

● Demonstrate the role of power, social status and prestige in determination of community decision-making.

● Stimulate consideration of the specifics of the participants' community and develop ideas for improving the effectiveness of community decision-making.

● Demonstrate how individuals work in groups to exert power.

● Help participants gain skills for their work in communities.

Preliminary instructions for game director

1. Plan the game in advance so that the details of play are clear to you.

2. Be sure to allow a minimum of three or four hours for playing the game. The game and analysis of the play could easily extend beyond this time by allowing more time for group analysis and discussion. It is possible to break up the time into two two-hour units.

3. Divide the participants into the spokesman groups — Business, Minority Groups, Homeowners Association, Coalition for Better Government, Church Groups and the City Council — around the room. Give each

group a briefing sheet for its group and ask it to discuss the viewpoints and interests of the group. If additional players are available, they may play the role of the Mass Media.

4. Clarify the time sequence of 20-minute units. This is the only period when spokesman groups can work with other groups to develop and obtain support for projects.

5. It is helpful to have a chalkboard or newsprint at a central place in the room where people may write their proposals. If this is not possible, players must work out their own communication systems with other groups.

6. Each spokesman group will need:

a. An identified place to meet.

b. A briefing sheet.

c. Pencils and paper to prepare its proposals, to allocate power points and to prepare press releases.

d. If a mass media group is included, it is helpful for it to have paper or newsprint, felt pens or crayons to prepare news bulletins. If these are not available, the gamesmaster may simply call for silence during a time sequence so that the mass media may give a short newscast. These should be limited to no more than three newscasts during a time sequence.

Participants' instructions

The primary purpose of "Community" is to experience the use of power by various groups within a community. You will be a member of a spokesman group representing citizens who respond to different needs and concerns in the community. The six spokesman groups are: Business, Minority Groups, Homeowners Association, Coalition for Better Government, Church Groups and the City Council. Each group, except the City Council, is allocated influence points. These points may be used to get proposals passed that will improve the community in the direction that they feel is important.

Game time is divided into 20-minute segments. During each of the 20-minute segments it is the responsibility of the spokesman groups to develop proposals and attempt to get them passed by the other groups and funded by the City Council. After

each round of play a rating of the influence points will be made, plus a vote of support or non-support for the City Council. After these have been tabulated, you will learn the consequences of the decisions that you and the other spokesman groups made. Then a new period begins, and you make a new set of proposals and decisions.

Time sequence

1. Groups develop proposals for improving the community and communicate them to other groups either by written messages, by placing them on a central board, or by sending a messenger to each of the other groups.

2. After 20 minutes the game director will distribute and collect decision forms for the groups to allocate their power points.

3. A tabulation of the points is made. To be approved, a proposal must receive a total of 50 points and the endorsement of the City Council. Points for a proposal are cumulative and are added after every time sequence. Allow some time for groups to discuss the results of the play period, and then repeat the sequence of events for at least four additional rounds of play.

BRIEFING SHEET FOR CITY COUNCIL

You have been elected by the citizens of Community to carry out the governmental activities. In the past, the City Council has given leadership to Community by identifying problems and working with groups to obtain support for constructive proposals.

You will vote upon every proposal and may approve it or veto it. Each action of the City Council is known. A key consideration is maintaining enough support so that you may be re-elected.

In planning your role and strategy, consider:

1) What are the primary concerns of your City Council and what kinds of proposals do you wish to develop?

2) Which groups and proposals are you going to support?

3) What strategies will you use?

4) What will be your response to other proposals?

BRIEFING SHEET FOR BUSINESS

The business sector of Community is most visible in the manufacturing industries which comprise 40% of all business enterprises. Service industries make up the remainder of the business community. The business sector has supported an intensive campaign to attract new industries to Community. This has been partially successful in that three small companies have located here.

In planning your role and strategy for the game, think through the following questions:

1) What are the primary concerns of business and what kinds of proposals do you wish to develop?

2) Which groups and proposals are you going to support?

3) What strategies will you use?

4) What will be your response to other proposals?

BRIEFING SHEET FOR COALITION FOR BETTER GOVERNMENT

Four years ago the Coalition for Better Government was formed by a group of concerned citizens. The primary purpose for organising was to react to problems caused by the attraction of new business to the community. Substandard housing, overcrowded schools, overtaxed city facilities and services were the primary problems accompanying a rapid growth in population. The coalition has been effective in organising public and private housing efforts and its positive influence has been felt in many other areas. The past experience of members in professional activities and in voluntary associations has given the coalition a commitment toward rational problem solving and practical solutions.

In planning your role and strategy consider:

1) What are the primary concerns of coalition and what kinds of proposals do you wish to develop?

2) Which groups and proposals are you going to support?

3) What strategies will you use?

4) What will be your response to other proposals?

BRIEFING SHEET FOR HOMEOWNERS ASSOCIATION

The Homeowners Association is made up of property owners who have worked very actively to maintain property values and obtain effective services from the city. Your primary concerns have been rising taxes and inadequate city services for garbage collection, street paving, police protection, etc. In the past the Homeowners Association has expressed great concern about the rapid population increase brought about by the location of new industries.

In planning your role and strategy, consider:

1) What are the primary concerns of the Homeowners Association and what kinds of proposals do you wish to develop?

2) Which groups and proposals are you going to support?

3) What strategies will you use?

4) What will be your response to other proposals?

BRIEFING SHEET FOR CHURCH GROUPS

The church groups in Community are just beginning to work together as an effective unit. During the crisis caused by a cyclone in another part of the country, the church groups successfully mobilised services for emergency housing, clothing and food. Since this time, they have continued to meet together to share concerns and work on problems. A major difficulty for the group has been obtaining endorsement for action from individual churches.

In planning your role and strategy, consider:

1) What are the primary concerns of church groups and what kinds of proposals do you wish to develop?,

2) Which groups and proposals are you going to support?

3) What strategies will you use?

4) What will be your response to other proposals?

BRIEFING SHEET FOR MINORITY GROUPS

Minority groups are not characterised by a single unified group. The most effective voice for minorities has been the School Improvement Council, organised several years ago to improve the quality of education for children. In recent years, it has expanded its concerns to housing, welfare payments, medical cases and other issues affecting the lives of its members.

In planning your role and strategy, consider:

1) What are the primary concerns of minority groups and what kinds of proposals do you wish to develop?

2) Which groups and proposals are you going to support?

3) What strategies will you use?

4) What will be your response to other proposals?

BRIEFING SHEET FOR MASS MEDIA

The mass media in Community (press, radio and TV) are owned by two national networks, but the general approach has been determined by station managers and editors. For this reason a variety of viewpoints has been available to citizens.

You may determine any philosophy or approach you wish to use. You may choose to support one group consistently or be responsive to all groups. You may be friendly, hostile, unfair or cooperative, as long as you disseminate the news.

Plan your role by considering:

1) What methods are you going to use to communicate with groups? (Central chalkboard or newsprint, short newscasts, papers to each group, etc.)

2) How are you going to gather news from the groups?

3) What strategy will you use for presenting the news?

QUESTIONS

How many influence points do we have?

Influence points are distributed in this way:

Business	20 points
Homeowners Association	20 points
Coalition for Better Government	20 points
Minority Groups	15 points
Church Groups	15 points
City Council	None

What is the role of the City Council?

The Council must approve or veto every proposal. A proposal can be taken to the City Council only after it has received 50 influence points. The Council may initiate proposals and meet with other groups to obtain their support and influence points.

What is the role of the mass media?

It is the role of the mass media to report the news and to disseminate information. They may call upon you or your group for information, or you or your group may wish to make press releases. Remember, however, that the mass media have total control over news coverage. They may or may not disseminate your press release, and will slant the news according to their own bias.

How are groups supposed to organise themselves?

Groups may organise themselves in any way they desire. Some groups elect a convenor, others rotate the responsibility. Some groups assign members of their group as liaisons with other groups.

Can proposals be amended?

A proposal can be amended only if the sponsoring group agrees to this.

How many time sequences are there?

It is wise to plan not less than four sequences but others may be added if the group so wishes.

How do power points accumulate?

Power points assigned to a proposal are cumulative from one time sequence to another. Power points, either positive or negative, may be assigned to a proposal during any time sequence. A total listing of points is tallied after each time sequence.

When has a proposal been passed?

When a proposal has received 50 positive points either during one time sequence or a number of sequences **and** it has obtained approval by the City Council, the proposal has passed.

Can groups vote against proposals?

Yes, each group may allocate its power points for (+) or against (−) proposals. For example, Business may allocate its 20 power points as +20 for a proposal. The Homeowners Association might vote −10 power points against that proposal. The proposal would then have +10 power points toward passage.

Can a proposal be defeated once it has passed?

Yes, if +50 power points are voted toward rescinding the proposal.

TABULATION OF POWER POINTS

Proposals*	1st Period	2nd Period	3rd Period	4th Period	5th Period	6th Period

*To pass, a proposal must receive +50 points and obtain approval from the City Council.

Analyse your community

Now that you've played "Community", use the following questions to analyse the use of power in your community.

1. Which are the spokesman groups in your community that have effectively used their power to act?

2. Which are the potential spokesman groups in your community that could contribute to the community if they developed their powers?

3. How is influence divided among groups in your community?

4. What are the characteristics of the spokesman groups in your community?

    a. City Council
    b. Business
    c. Minority Groups
    d. Homeowners
    e. Coalition
    f. Mass Media
    g. Other

5. What proposals have each of the spokesman groups initiated in your community? What proposals would they support?

6. What strategies have groups used to act in your community?

7. What strategies can **your** group use in your community?

8. What is the communications pattern in your community?

SPIEL

A game designed by Michael Hammill-Green

Spiel is a simple board game for up to eight players, designed to help people think and talk about subjects of group interest, share points of view, and become better acquainted. It may be used to open up and/or summarise a particular topic, or to hear opinions on a variety of topics. The game designer developed this game to use in Social Studies classes.

Materials

The design of the playing board may be in any shape : square, triangle, Z-shape, etc. A design similar to that of Monopoly might be easiest. It should have 30—40 squares, plus a start and finish. You will need space for the stack of Spiel Cards. Put about ten "S Card" squares on the board, and five "Challenge" squares.

Stack of Spiel Cards (copies onto systems cards)

Dice

Tokens

Stopwatch

Playing the game

1. The first one to reach "Finish" is the winner.

2. Each player advances by throwing the die (one of the pair of dice). There is no repeat throw following a six.

3. Players landing on an "S Card" square pick up a Spiel Card. After a maximum of 30 seconds for thinking, the player speaks on the topic indicated.

4. Players unable to speak for at **least 60 seconds** on the topic must **go back 1 space**. A pause of 5 seconds shall be considered the end of the spiel.

5. Players who succeed in speaking for at least 60 seconds **go forward 1 space.**

6. Players who succeed in speaking for at least 2 minutes **go forward two spaces.**

7. Players who succeed in speaking for three or more minutes **go forward three spaces.**

8. Players may refuse one card drawn and take another, but if any further cards are refused, the player must **go back one space** per card refused.

9. Players who land on a "Challenge" square may challenge one other player to speak for two minutes on a topic nominated by the challenger. If the challenge is refused, the challenger **goes forward two spaces.** If the challenged player accepts and succeeds in speaking for two minutes, he **goes forward two spaces.**

Spiel cards *(adapt or replace as appropriate)*

Should smoking be allowed at school?

My favourite sport is . . .

Pie and sauce is better than pizza because . . .

Eating people is wrong because . . .

The best television show is . . . (say why).

If I were running (insert name of school), I would . . .

When I leave school, I will . . .

Men are worse drivers than women.

Drinking while driving is a crime.

The girls I dislike most are . . .

The girls I like most are . . .

In a hundred years, the world will be . . .

I do or don't believe in ghosts and other supernatural events.

Will Mohammed Ali win his next fight?

Is there life on other planets?

Does God exist?

Prisons should be torn down.

School is a waste of time.

Police pick on teenagers.

Skinheads cause trouble.

If I were Prime Minister, I would . . .

Communism means . . .

Sex before marriage is wrong.

Colour television is a waste of money.

Do workers get a fair go in Australia?

Trade unions are a good thing.

Too much money makes you just as unhappy as too little money.

The best film I've seen is . . . (say why).

Are women superior to men?

Is hanging wrong?

Aboriginals should be given back their land.

The most dangerous moment in my life was when I . . .

If I won $10,000 in Tattslotto, I would . . .

R Certificate censorship of films and books should be continued.

Australia has benefited from having migrants.

Should wearing a seat-belt be compulsory?

Is space research a waste of money?

Is alcohol more dangerous than marijuana?

Should smoking marijuana be allowed?

Should smoking be banned?

Is homosexuality a crime?

Should corporal punishment be used at school?

If you can live okay on the dole, why bother working?

The places I've enjoyed going to most are . . . (say why).

The thing I spend most time on outside school is . . .

Motor bikes are more dangerous than cars.

My favourite rock group is . . . (say why).

I like people who . . .

I hate people who . . .

The most exciting moment in my life was . . .

The most embarrassing moment in my life was . . .

The person I admire most is . . .

GROUP 5

A game for 15 or more players by Ian Louttit

Purpose

This game is intended to highlight the feelings of group acceptance and rejection.

Rules

1. Each player aims to earn as many points as possible during the course of the game.

2. The game is divided into 10 x 3-minute rounds with progress points being marked on a chalkboard at the end of each round.

3. No talking is allowed during the game by anyone except the game director.

4. In each round players will group together according to conditions on the backs of players. Players are unaware of the conditions on their own backs. The maximum size of groups to be formed is 5. This earns maximum points for each player in the group. In every round some people will be rejected and will lose points.

Procedure

1. Before the game, prepare a condition tag for each person, following the instructions below. Pin a tag on the back of each player. Make it clear that PLAYERS ARE NOT ALLOWED TO READ THEIR OWN TAGS.

2. Explain to the players that the idea of the game is to score the most points possible over the ten rounds by forming into groups of up to five people. The scoring will be as follows:

Group of 5 — 5 points to each player in the group
Group of 4 — 2 points each
Group of 3 — 1 point each
Group of 2 — no points
Lone players — minus 1 point

If a group does not comply with all conditions, each player loses 10 points.

3. Before grouping with others, check their condition tags to see if they are acceptable. This must be done in silence. No one is to be told what condition they have on their back.

4. When someone is found who is acceptable to your group for that round, link arms to indicate a group forming.

5. The game director clearly indicates the beginning of each round and the number of the round. At the end of each round he/she calls time. Scores for the round are noted and progress scores posted.

Condition tags

1. Reject this person for rounds 1 to 5, then accept any time.

2. Reject this person for rounds 1 and 2, then accept any time.

3. Reject this person if younger than you. If uncertain, reject.

4. Reject this person after round 3 and for remainder of game.

5. Reject this person after round 4 and for remainder of game.

6. Reject this person if shorter than you. (Don't make measuring obvious.)

7. Reject this person if taller than you. (Don't make measuring obvious.)

8. Never reject this person.

9. Reject this person in rounds 2, 4 and 6.

10. Reject this person in rounds 1, 3, 6, 9 and 10.

11. Reject this person if wearing the same colour shirt/blouse as you.

12. Reject this person after round 4 and for remainder of game.

13. Reject this person in rounds 1 and 2, then accept any time.

14. Reject this person if he/she has been in your group more than once.

15. Reject this person in rounds 5, 7, 9 and 10.

16. Reject this person if you haven't met his/her parents.

17. Reject this person in rounds 1 to 3, then accept any time.

18. Reject this person in rounds 4, 7 and 9.

19. Reject this person if he/she is looking sad or serious.

20. Reject this person if he/she has been in your group more than twice.

If there are more than twenty players, you may start again at No. 1, or make up some of your own.

Debriefing

After the game:

- Discuss points scored by the players.
- Could the players determine why they were being rejected?
- What were players' feelings when rejected continually? What were their feelings when they were accepted at first and then rejected?
- Did anyone really feel secure?
- How did players feel towards those never rejected?
- Was it difficult to choose the last member of the group?
- Did the fact that it was non-verbal affect the players?
- In what ways does the game resemble reality?

FACE TO FACE

Face to Face is a card game designed to stimulate personal sharing between people who already know each other at least superficially.

Face to Face is played by two, three or four people. More than one game can be played in the same room at the same time. Each game needs a deck of cards. Each player receives all the cards of the same suit, excepting the jack. Thus, one player has spades, another hearts, another clubs, etc. Jacks, jokers, and plain cards are not used.

For two players the game is played as follows:

1.   The players sit face to face, preferably across a table or on the floor.

2.   The first player says a sentence expressing an attitude about something. (It need not be his own attitude.) These statements may describe **emotions,** for example, "I feel fine when I am alone", **opinions** like, "I am against capital punishment", **reactions,** for example, "I blush when someone praises me", **tastes or preferences** such as, "I like working out of doors", **values,** "I feel it's more important to have a good reputation than to be rich", or **beliefs,** such as, "I believe in life after death."

3.   Each player indicates his position on the statement made by choosing a card between one (the ace) and ten. He or she chooses the card from 1 to 10 on this basis:

1 indicates:	total disagreement
2 or 3 indicates:	strong disagreement
4 or 5 indicates:	slight disagreement
6 or 7 indicates:	slight agreement
8 or 9 indicates:	strong agreement
10 indicates:	total agreement

The player places this card face down to his/her left.

4.   For this same statement, each player chooses a card which he believes corresponds with the position taken by the other player, that is, the card the other player has chosen. The player places this second card face down to his/her right. Each player now has a "me" card to the left and a "you" card to the right.

5.   The players turn over the cards taking care not to reverse the positions.

6.   Each player counts his points by noting the difference between the cards on his right (that is, the card by which he described the other's position, and the card the opposite player actually played). For example, in the diagram, John and Louise are playing Face to Face. John places a 9 to his right, thinking that Louise strongly agreed with the statement. Louise, however, has rated her own position with a 5. John's score is 4. Meanwhile, Louise has estimated John's position as 8, while he rated himself on 7. Louise's score is 1.

7.   The players note their scores for this round.

8.   The players take back their cards, and the second player makes a statement which could describe an attitude. Once again, each player lays down two cards: to the left for "me", to the right for "you".

9.   Points are counted the same way as before, and added to the previous score.

10.   If a player prefers not to reveal his position on the statement given, or to guess the position of the opposite player, he puts down a king or queen. The score for that player is then the highest of all other cards on the table for that particular round. For example, John prefers not to reveal his position on a particular statement. He puts a queen to his left, and his score is 8, the highest card showing.

If there are three players, one person makes a statement and the other two play Face to Face. Then the next person makes a statement and the two others play, and so on. If there are four players, the two people playing Face to Face add up their points. As a couple, they play "against" the other couple. The lowest score wins.

The first person to reach 50 points, or the first couple to reach 100 points, loses the game. Of course, the better you know someone, the lower your score is likely to be.

Questions for discussion

1. Were you surprised at the accuracy or inaccuracy of your answers?

2. Did you learn anything about yourself?

3. Did you learn anything about anyone else?

4. What does winning mean in this game? What does losing mean?

5. What surprised you the most in the game?

6. Which attitude areas (emotions, opinions, reactions, tastes, values, beliefs) did you choose to speak in most often? Why?

7. In which attitude areas did you score best (that is, lowest)? What does this help you recognise about yourself?

8. Did the game make personal sharing easier?

EXPRESSING FEELINGS

A simple card game for 4 to 10 players

Purpose:

To help participants to express their feelings, and to see that their signals are sometimes misunderstood by others.

Materials needed:

- An ordinary pack of playing cards, with jokers removed.

- A sheet of newsprint or a chalkboard with the numbers 2 to 10 and jack, queen, king, ace written down one side.

To play:

1. The group draws up a list of thirteen feelings or emotions, one beside each number. (If you wish, this can be done ahead of time by the leader.)

2. One player starts by dealing four cards to each player. The remainder of the cards are placed face down in the middle of the group.

3. The player on the dealer's left compares his/her cards with the list of feelings. Maybe he has a 4 which is listed as "warmth", a 7 which is "joy", and 8 "loneliness", and a queen "love". He must mime **one** of those feelings for others in the group to guess. Say he chooses "loneliness". He places the 8 face down in front of him and proceeds to mime the feeling.

4. Others in the group who think they know the feeling being mimed, and who also hold the corresponding card (in this case the 8), place that card face down in front of them.

5. The first player then turns his card face up, and the others who have put down cards do the same.

6. If at least one of the others guessed correctly, the first player puts his card on the bottom of the discard pile. If not, he takes the card back into his hand, and takes an additional card from the top of the discard pile.

7. All the players who guessed correctly put their cards on the bottom of the discard pile. If they were wrong they retain the card and take an additional card from the top of the discard pile.

8. The same procedure is followed for each player in turn. The object is to get rid of all one's cards.

9. With a smaller group (e.g., four or five) it would be better to deal a greater number of cards, say about eight. You can adjust the number of cards dealt to suit the size of the group, always remembering that you need to start with a discard pile of about ten cards. With more than ten players, use two packs, or divide into two groups for two separate games.

Afterwards:

- Invite participants to talk about their reactions to the game and to the other players, particularly with regard to any frustrations they experienced.

- Talk about ways of making signals of emotion and feeling easier to understand. What helps this? What hinders this, or causes misunderstanding?

PIONEER

An adaptation of the NASA exercise by Mary-Ruth Marshall

Pioneer is a role-playing game in which participants put themselves in the place of the pioneers and colonists of Australia's early days. This highlights life styles of the present day, so drastically changed from those of the 1700s. In addition, players experience the process of group decision-making in comparison to individual decision-making.

Players

Any number of players may play the game, in groups of about eight. A minimum of five to ten participants is needed for an effective game.

Materials

- Copies of the supply list (see below)
- Paper
- Pencils

Playing the Game

1. Players should sit in a circle around a table or on the floor. Five to ten players make up a family.

2. Read this scenario to all players: "The time is the 1700s. Your group is an English family who has decided to emmigrate to Australia. You are going to be pioneers in the area opening up inland. As a family, you are trying to make a list of twenty items that will be most useful to you in your new setting. You will have to take the items with you or buy them in Sydney after landing. You have made a list but now need to narrow it down to twenty items. Each one of you, with no assistance from the other group members, is now to make a list of the twenty most useful items for the life of a settler. Space and transport is not a deciding factor — what cannot be sent by ship will be bought in Sydney — but you have to make your list now."

3. Individually, players complete their lists, ranking the items from 1 to 20 in order of their usefulness or importance.

4. When each participant has completed his list, the family as a group seeks consensus in deciding the twenty most useful items for the family to have on the frontier. This means that all family (group) members must agree on the necessity and ranking of each item before it becomes part of the family decision.

5. Compare the final decisions of the entire group to the lists of individual members. Share lists between families.

D

Debriefing

1. Who reached the better decisions — the group working together or individuals on their own? Why?

2. How did this activity help you identify with the life of the early settler?

3. What understanding does this game give to your awareness of contemporary values and life styles?

4. What behaviours were helpful in reaching consensus agreement? What behaviours were not helpful?

5. What did you learn about cooperation which will be helpful in future tasks?

SUPPLY LIST

iron pot	candles	iron frypan
horse	cow	pigs
lead	flint	spade
axe	sugar	bullet mould
gun powder	salt	Bible
compass	plow	bull
chickens	churn	hoe
treacle	cheese	saw
scythe	musket	fish hooks
fish net	spinning wheel	seeds
candle mould	table and chairs	dried herbs
pewter utensils	wooden bowls	harness
barrel of salt pork	bushels of wheat	dried beans
wagon	rope	

YELLOW SUBMARINE

A game for any number of players
by Fred Doscher

From Dennis Benson's *Recycle Catalogue* (Abingdon Press, 1975). Used by permission.

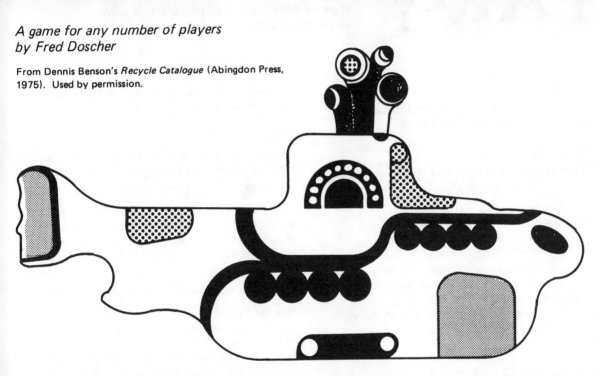

The Beatle record "Yellow Submarine" is a handy resource for group building and discussing values. We were talking about things important to us and decided that as part of our camp we would do a thing on the end of the world. The submarine would be our shelter. So we played the record with the lights real low. We showed slides of ocean and underwater life. We then gave the instructions for the experience: "We must abandon land. Atomic fallout has ruined the soil, and contamination is coming from the ground and air. We are a small group with a submarine available. We can take on board, for our lives together, only what will fit in the submarine." We drew the outline of a submarine on paper, big enough for a group to sit squatted but with little room to move. We suggested that we could bring what would fit between our feet and around us. There would be fifteen minutes before departure time. We had recorded the Beatles' song so that it would play over and over again for fifteen minutes.

When the time was over, the paper was covered. We used magazine pictures of actual objects and animals and people we would bring (symbolic). Room had to be left for foot contact with the paper.

We sang along with the Beatles when the time was up. After the experience we hung our "production" (paper submarine) on the wall and shared reactions. We thought it was important to make a graph of items, and to begin to study our life style and what kind of life style we desire and what kind we could afford in the new context.

The intriguing thing was that the group made an observation about what they were bringing. We could last about a month with the things we had chosen. The discussion ended by brainstorming new kinds of food and mind resources that would help us keep alive mentally and spiritually. The list revealed a great deal about the nature of the people in our community.

PARTY

by Coralie N. Ling

A game designed for 23 players, but with variation possible

Purpose:

To create awareness of sex roles and the advantages and disadvantages of maintaining them.

Playing time:

30 minutes, followed by at least 30 minutes discussion.

Setting:

A party at the home of Jack and Jill.

Materials needed:

a large name tag and role definition for each player
a bowl from which the roles are drawn
a bell to mark the end of each round
drinks (to be served at the end of each round)
background music for atmosphere

Rules

1. Each person must keep within his/her role but can act very freely within it.

2. The host and hostess serve drinks at the end of each round. Players are to take a drink only if they are enjoying the party.

Procedure

1. The game director explains the purpose, setting and rules of the game.

2. Each person draws a piece of paper (role description) from the bowl and then finds the corresponding name tag. (It is the luck of the draw whether players have male or female roles.)

3. The game director rings a bell to indicate the beginning of round one and the host and hostess greet their guests. Those players who are to enter the party later wait at the door.

4. Each round lasts 5 minutes. The game director rings the bell to indicate the end of the round and the host and hostess serve drinks.

5. There are five rounds. At the end of the fifth round, all leave.

Roles

There are five traditional male roles and five traditional female roles, making a basic core group of ten.

KEN/STEWART/BOB/PETER/DAVID

You are a traditional man. You are married to . . . . . , a traditional woman. You want to enjoy the party. You mix with the boys, like beer, discuss football, work, cars, etc. If the party is really terrible you could find an excuse to leave.

CAROL/SUSAN/HELEN/MARY/ELIZABETH

You are a traditional woman. You are married to . . . , a traditional man. You want to enjoy the party. You mix with the women and discuss women's issues — babies, clothes, home decorating, etc. If the party is really terrible you could find an excuse to leave.

The other roles are designed to bring different dynamics into the party.

JACK

You are the host of the party. You want everyone to enjoy themselves. You try to keep everything easy-going and keep the drink flowing at the end of each round. After each round you discuss with Jill (your wife) how you think the party is going.

JILL

You are the hostess of the party. You want everyone to enjoy the party. You try to calm any disagreement. You bring round drinks at the end of each round. Then you discuss with Jack (your husband) how you think the party is going.

FRED

Your are rapt in your wife Fran. You will not separate from her and just want to talk to her, but you will try to be sociable.

FRAN

You are concerned only with your husband Fred. You will not leave him alone. You just want to talk with him, though you will try to be sociable.

BARRY

You usually play the traditional male role. Your wife Barbara has just had a new baby and you help in the house for the first time. You have brought the baby to the party and he is sleeping in the main bedroom.

BARBARA

You play the traditional woman's role and have a new baby with you at the party. (He is sleeping in the main bedroom.) Your husband Barry is very taken with the novelty of a baby. He is helping in the house for the first time.

JOHN

You are a traditional male. Your wife Joan often flirts with other men. This makes you very angry. At the party you would prefer to talk to the boys, but you have to keep an eye on what Joan is up to.

JOAN

You are out for flirtation and adventure with the boys. Your husband John is a traditional male and will be jealous if you flirt, otherwise he will ignore you.

MANFRED

You and your wife Margaret are a non-traditional couple. You try to get the party playing some different games. You talk to the opposite sex about roles, marriage, radical politics. You find the going difficult and leave at the end of round three.

MARGARET

You and your husband Manfred are a non-traditional couple. You try to get the party playing some different games. You talk to the opposite sex about roles, marriage, radical politics. You find the going difficult and leave after round three.

PATRICIA

You are a women's libber. You want to get men and women mixing and discussing important issues together — education, politics, women's roles in society. You persist very strongly in your goals at the party. You enter the party after round one.

ALBERT

You are a near alcoholic, dominated by your wife Anne. You give in to her over everything except drink. She drives the car, manages the finances, etc. You enter the party after round two.

ANNE

You are very moral. You dominate your husband Albert. You always drive the car, manage the finances, etc. Your husband is a near alcoholic. He gives in to you over everything except drink. You enter the party after round two.

If extra roles are needed you could add more traditional couples, plus some others, e.g., engaged couple, lone wolf, divorcee looking for a new husband, couple living together though not married, gate-crashers, etc.

Progress of the party: *(For game director's use only)*

ROUND ONE	The party begins. Jack and Jill welcome guests: the five traditional couples, Barbara and Barry (and baby) Joan and John, Fran and Fred, Manfred and Margaret.
ROUND TWO	Patricia, the women's libber, arrives and begins to stir things.
ROUND THREE	Ann and Albert arrive.
ROUND FOUR	Manfred and Margaret leave. When they do, game director sends them back with a problem — their car is bogged and they need help to shift it.
ROUND FIVE	At some time during this round, game director announces that Barbara's and Barry's baby is having convulsions.
	All leave.

Debriefing and discussion

At the conclusion of the game, ask the players to remove their name tags and sit in a circle to discuss the game. Discussion might centre at first on what happened in the game, how people felt about what happened, and how they felt about their roles. Then it might be broadened to look at sex roles in society and at the problems and possibilities involved in breaking away from traditional roles.

THE Game of life

Two suggestions for using the commercially produced (John Sands) board game, "Life"

SUGGESTION ONE

We have worked up a simulation experience using "Life". Additional rules and regulations have been designed to place the game into a real-life Christian context where game decisions are made as if they were actual living situations. In this context the "game" offers some stimulating choices and discussions on the influence of the Christian faith on vocational choices, ethics, family responsibilities, community relations and witness to the faith.

Rules and procedures

1. One player will be the moderator of the game.

2. The game is to be played realistically as if the decisions made are true to life and decisions that would be made in the individual's life choices.

3. Each player can challenge the moves made by the other players. If the majority of the players decide that the move made by any other player is inconsistent with that individual's life style, personality and goals, then the player in question will forfeit one turn at play. Players have the right to respond to each challenge. Examples of decisions that might evoke a challenge: tertiary education; number of children; vocational choice.

4. A player may be asked at any time during his turn to comment on the influence of Christian faith on the game choice and decision made.

5. Game winner will be determined by who finishes first, and by their expression of the place of faith in their life's decisions in the game.

SUGGESTION TWO *by Brian Morgan*

The game of "Life" has a terribly materialistic philosophy and raises some good questions about values. By playing it you should be able to look at your values and the underlying assumptions of your life.

Play the game according to the rules. Then use these questions and activities to help the group reflect on the game:

- Which event did you find most exciting?

- At which point in the game were you most uncomfortable?

- List the underlying assumptions of the game. Discuss whether they are acceptable or not to you as a Christian.

- Talk about how you handled power in the game. Use this to look at some situations in your lives when you have been in positions of power, e.g. leadership positions, boy-girl relationships.

- Some people have life styles approximating that indicated by the assumptions of the game. How would you express God's word of hope to them? Role play a situation in which you declare the word of hope. Then, reflect with the players on it.

A game by Brian Morgan for any number of players

Purpose:

To look at dating dilemmas.

Number of players:

This is a game for any number of people, preferably playing in small groups of about 4.

A caution:

Since it is a game which involves real feelings, care should be taken to be supportive to people who find themselves in serious conflict between their convictions and their real life actions. You may need to watch for those who find themselves ridiculed or condemned by other players beyond their ability to cope.

Preparation:

1. Prepare a game board as illustrated. Draw it on a large sheet of newsprint to be placed on the floor in the middle of the room, or draw directly on the floor with chalk. It should be at least 1 metre by 2 metres.

2. Prepare as many copies of the situations as you expect to have small groups.

3. You will need a dice and a distinctive token for each group.

Instructions

1. Divide into small groups of 3 to 8 people (the best size is about 4 people). Give each group a pair of dice, token and copy of the situations. If you have less than 12 players, or want the game to last longer, use a single die.

2. Locate the groups spaced out around the game board so that they can discuss without disturbing the other groups.

3. At a signal from the game director, someone in each group throws the dice and places their token on the appropriate spot on the game board.

4. Members of each group turn to the situation which has the same number as the space where their token is located. They have three to five minutes (or as decided by the game director) to discuss the situation and to decide whether the action is appropriate or inappropriate, in their opinion. Appropriate action is rewarded (e.g. "Go forward 1"); inappropriate action receives a penalty (e.g. "Go back 2"). (Some "situations" appear in two forms, (a) and (b). The members of each group choose the form which appears most real to them, unless instructed otherwise by the game director.)

5. The game director calls time and the groups in turn report the situation and their decision, including significant reasons. They then make the reward or penalty move according to their decision. If they decided the action was appropriate, they move forward. If they felt it was inappropriate, they move backward.

6. When all have moved, the next round begins with all groups simultaneously throwing the dice again. Continue until a team reaches 30 (THE WINNER).

7. The first group to reach THE WINNER opens discussion on the question, "What have you really won?" This should not be allowed to drag. It is only meant as a summing up of the learnings of the individual situations.

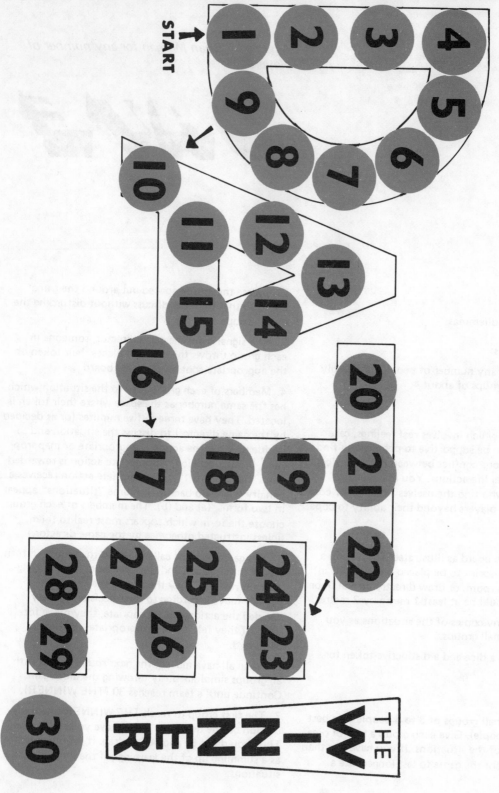

THE WIZZER

START

1 2 3 4 5 6 7 8 9 10 11 12 13 14 15 16 17 18 19 20 21 22 23 24 25 26 27 28 29 30

The situations

1. You dance all evening with your own partner at the Youth Club Ball. START AGAIN OR GO FORWARD 1.

2. You think that at 16 you should be allowed to stay out until 2.00 a.m. if you want to. START AGAIN OR GO FORWARD 2.

3. You hear a joke which you don't understand but it has something to do with sex, so you ask for an explanation. There is an embarrassed silence but you repeat your request. GO BACK 2 OR GO FORWARD 2.

4. (a) Your "steady" of two months is unbuttoning your shirt. You ask her to stop.
(b) Your "steady" of two months is unbuttoning your blouse. You ask him to stop and to take you home. THROW THE DICE. GO BACKWARDS OR FORWARDS BY THE NUMBER THROWN.

5. (a) You leave your own date all alone at the party and spend all night "chatting up" another girl.
(b) You leave your own date all alone at the party and spend all night flirting with another guy. GO BACKWARDS 2 OR GO FORWARDS 2.

6. You ask your parents to stay home and host your 18th birthday party. GO BACKWARDS OR FORWARDS THE NUMBER OF YOUR LAST THROW.

7. You brag exaggeratedly to your mates about "how far you got" on Saturday night. GO BACKWARDS OR FORWARDS BY THE NUMBER OF PEOPLE IN YOUR GROUP.

8. (a) Your girl friend is pregnant. You are both 18. You had no intention of marrying but you decide to "under the circumstances".
(b) You are pregnant. You are both 18. You had no intention of marrying but you decide to "under the circumstances". GO BACKWARDS 2 OR FORWARDS 2.

9. (a) It has been a real groovy first night out. You thank him and kiss him lightly on the lips.
(b) It has been a real groovy first night out. You thank her and kiss her lightly on the lips. GO BACKWARDS 3 OR FORWARDS 3.

10. (a) You are going out with a very pleasant girl. She is not thought by your peer group to be very good looking and they stir you about it. You drop her cold.
(b) You are going out with a very interesting guy. He is not thought by your peer group to be very good looking and they stir you about it. You drop him cold. GO BACKWARDS OR FORWARDS BY THE NUMBER OF GROUPS.

11. You have accepted an invitation from someone you really don't like, to see a film that you really want to see. GO BACKWARDS 2 OR FORWARDS 2.

12. (a) Her reputation is "easy" so you ask her out to "get your share".
(b) His reputation is "fast" so you ask him out "for the experience". GO BACKWARDS OR FORWARDS 4.

13. You are sitting with a group of fairly close friends at the party when one of them pulls out some grass and suggest you all share a joint. You refuse and leave the group. THROW THE DICE. MOVE BACKWARDS OR FORWARDS BY THE NUMBER THROWN.

14. (a) You refuse her request to take her parking.
(b) You refuse his request to go parking.
GO BACKWARDS 3 OR FORWARDS 3.

15. (a) It is your first time out and he wants to walk holding hands. You refuse politely.
(b) It is your first time out and she wants to walk holding hands. You refuse politely.
GO BACKWARDS 1 OR FORWARDS 1.

16. (a) You decide to carry sheath contraceptives in the glovebox of your car — "just in case".
(b) You decide to take the pill — "just in case".
DECIDE YOUR OWN PENALTY OR REWARD. EXPLAIN YOUR DECISION.

17. It is midnight. You should be home, but the party is just getting warmed up. You decide to stay. GO BACKWARDS 5 OR FORWARDS 5.

18. Mum asks you to bring your date in to meet the family. You refuse. GO BACKWARDS 3 OR FORWARDS 3.

19. (a) A guy you don't really want to get serious with asks you out. You accept. On the morning of the date a guy you are crazy over rings up and asks you out that night. You accept and phone the first guy and tell him that your parents won't let you go out.
(b) You have asked a girl out who is keen on you but you do not want to get serious. On the morning of the date you meet a fantastic "old flame" so you ask her out that night, then phone the first girl and tell her you have been confined to the house by

your parents. GO BACKWARDS OR FORWARDS BY THE NUMBER OF PEOPLE IN YOUR GROUP.

20.　He is married but great fun, so you accept his offer for a lift home — and coffee and a cuddle on the way. GO BACKWARDS OR FORWARDS BY THE NUMBER OF PEOPLE IN YOUR GROUP.

21.　(a) After six dates he hasn't tried anything more than a gentle kiss. You tell him he is uninterestingly slow.

　　　(b) You tell her that after six dates she ought to be prepared to allow petting. GO BACKWARD OR FORWARD THE NUMBER OF PEOPLE IN THE GROUP.

22.　Your date is a little drunk but insists on driving home so you ask another friend to drive you home from the party, leaving your date to make his own way home. GO BACKWARD 2 OR FORWARD 2.

23.　You phone to advise your parents that you will not be able to be home by the prearranged time. GO BACKWARD 3 OR FORWARD 3.

24.　You decline an invitation from a friend to join a lunchtime "orgy" at the home of another friend whose parents are away. THROW THE DICE — MOVE BACKWARD OR FORWARD THE NUMBER THROWN.

25.　You are both 18 and have been going together for two years. You jointly agree after discussion to have sexual intercourse. GO BACKWARD 4 OR FORWARD 4.

26.　No one has asked you to the local group's Ball but you want to go, so you phone up a guy in the group and ask him to come with you. CHOOSE YOUR OWN PENALTY OR REWARD. EXPLAIN YOUR DECISION.

27.　Someone suggests that the lights be turned out at a mixed party. You escape to the kitchen. GO BACKWARDS OR FORWARDS THE NUMBER OF YOUR LAST THROW.

28.　(a) You are not really interested in boys at all and would rather go out with your girl friends or stay at home, but your friends stir you about it. Finally you ask them to organise a date for you.

　　　(b) You are not really interested in girls at all and would rather go out with your mates or stay at home, but your friends stir you about it. Finally you ask them to organise a date for you. GO BACKWARDS 1 OR FORWARDS 1.

29.　(a) Your best mate is working to take your other mate's girl friend from him and telling you about it. You decide to expose the situation.

　　　(b) Your best friend is working to take your other friend's boy friend from her and telling you about it. You decide to expose the situation. GO BACKWARDS 2 OR FORWARDS to WINNER.

30.　You decide that sexual intercourse is out but mutual masturbation to orgasm is O.K. GO BACKWARDS 1 OR FORWARDS TO WINNER.

58

YOUTH IN THE CHURCH

A game for six or more players by Pat Baker

Purpose: To explore the position of young people in the local church, particularly in relation to

a) communication problems,
b) tensions between youth and the source of authority.

Instructions to the Game Director

1. Divide the players into two, three or four groups, depending on how many players you have. The first two groups — the Youth Group and the Parish Council — are essential to the game. The other two — the Council of Elders and Members of the Congregation — are optional. Each group needs at least three members. Locate the groups well away from one another. If your church is part of the Uniting Church in Australia, consult the *Constitution and Regulations* for the duties and responsibilities of the Parish Council (regulations 3.3.1 and 3.3.2) and the Council of Elders (regulation 3.1.9). The Parish Council is particularly concerned with administrative matters, including property and finance. The Council of Elders shares with the minister the spiritual oversight of the parish and the responsibility for worship, Christian education and evangelism. If you belong to a different religious denomination, you may prefer to change the two councils to something more familiar in your church.

2. Set the scene for the game. There are three churches in the Parish, but most activities other than worship are combined. The Parish Youth Group meets at the Central Church. There is one Council of Elders for the whole Parish. During the course of the game the players will be dealing with situations that arise in the life of the Parish. They will be asked to respond, not as themselves, but as they think members of their particular group would.

3. Suggest that, in order to establish their roles, each person now introduce himself/herself to the other members of his group in his new identity, giving a fictitious name, age, and one or two points of interest about himself. (Members of the Congregation should mainly be members of Central Church, but a few could be from South or West.)

4. Explain how the game is to be played (see below) and the time limits for each round. Give a set of score cards to each member of the Parish Council (and to each member of the Council of Elders and each Member of the Congregation). Answer questions for clarification.

5. Begin play. Give out the first situation outline to each group and announce that timing has begun. The Youth Group's outline includes possible courses of action. The groups have three minutes to discuss the situation among themselves. Members of the Youth Group must decide on their response.

6. Call time. A representative of the Youth Group reads the situation outline aloud and states the group's response.

7. Members of the Parish Council (and other groups) have three minutes to react. They must react individually within their own groups by each giving a score to the Youth Group. That is, if a member of the Parish Council thinks the Youth Group has responded well to the situation he/she shows a 5 card. The lower the value of the card, the less satisfaction with the response. The group's average is taken. If the average is less than 3, members prepare a spoken reaction, beginning, "You should have . . . "

8. Call time. Ask for the Parish Council reaction. If the average score has been 3 or more, a representative of the Council shows the appropriate score card, without speaking. If the score is lower than 3, the representative shows the appropriate score card and gives the spoken statement prepared by the group. Other adult groups report scores in the same way. Record the scores.

9. Give out the next set of situation outlines and follow the same pattern as for round one.

10. When all (or an agreed number) of the situations have been considered, announce the end of the game and total scores.

11. Ask the players to come into one group and abandon their group identities. Discuss the game and the issues it raises. Here are some possible points for discussion:

- What happened?
- How did you feel about the game?
- How did you feel about your group? About the other group(s)?
- Were you frustrated by the time limits?
- What did you think of the scoring system?
- Did you feel that the other groups really understood the situation?
- Is what happens in your church anything like what happened in the game?
- What is the place of young people in your church?

NOTE: Interaction between the groups is not suggested or encouraged, but it is not specifically prohibited. If someone takes such an initiative, let it go and see what happens.

Resources and materials

The Parish Council and Council of Elders will need an outline of their duties and responsibilities.

Each group will need a copy of each situation to be looked at. (See below.)

Each member of the Parish Council, the Council of Elders, and the Congregation needs a set of numbers (1—5) for scoring.

The game director needs a watch with a second hand for accurate timing.

Situation outlines

As you prepare to deal with each situation, give each group the appropriate copy. (Notice that the hand out is a little different for each group.)

SITUATION #1   YOUTH GROUP

Your group wants a place it can call its own. There is a small room adjoining the Central Church hall that no one ever uses. At present it's full of junk, but you could soon get it cleared out and cleaned up. Everyone is prepared to pitch in and you have plenty of ideas about how you want to decorate and furnish it.

Do you —

- ask the Parish Council for permission to take over the room?
- start cleaning out the junk?
- try to get the interest of some of the older people in the church?
- or what?

SITUATION #1   PARISH COUNCIL

You have been talking lately of making the best possible use of existing property. In particular you have been discussing uses for a small room adjoining the Central Church hall. At present it is used for storage, but many of the things in it are no longer wanted and could be disposed of. If the room were available it would be useful for small meetings.

SITUATION #1   COUNCIL OF ELDERS

The Parish Council has been looking into the best possible use of existing property. A small room adjoining the Central Church hall is being used for storage, but many of the things in it are no longer wanted and could be disposed of. If the room were available it would be useful for small meetings.

SITUATION #1   CONGREGATION

A small room adjoining the Central Church hall is being used for storage, but many of the things in it are no longer wanted and could be disposed of. If the room were available it could be used for small meetings.

SITUATION #2   YOUTH GROUP

You want to start a regular contemporary worship service at Central Church. In the past there has been an occasional "youth service" but it's been planned by the minister and you haven't been given much opportunity to contribute.

Do you —

- arrange for a few people to talk it over with the minister?
- send a delegation to the Parish Council to explain what you have in mind?
- plan a "pilot" service with the idea of winning support?
- give up and go to another church that already has contemporary worship?
- or what?

SITUATION #2   PARISH COUNCIL

Most of the worship services in the Parish are fairly traditional. However, the minister has occasionally arranged a "youth service" in which the young people have done the readings and some modern hymns have been used. You hear that some of the young people want more contemporary services and that they want to have more of a hand in the planning.

SITUATION #2   COUNCIL OF ELDERS

Most of the worship services in the Parish are fairly traditional. However, the minister has occasionally arranged a "youth service" in which the young people have done the readings and some modern hymns have been used. The young people seem less enthusiastic about this than you would have expected.

SITUATION #2   CONGREGATION

Most of the worship services in the Parish are fairly traditional. However, the minister has occasionally arranged a "youth service" in which the young people have done the readings and some modern hymns have been used. Some of the young people have been saying that they want regular "rock" services.

SITUATION #3   YOUTH GROUP

The Youth Group really got into working for the Christmas Bowl last year and raised far more than anyone else in the Parish. Everyone said "well done" at the time, but now they seem to have forgotten who did all the hard work and are patting themselves on the back because the Parish raised so much money.

Do you —

- refuse to organize anything this year?
- ask members of some of the other groups in the Parish to meet with you to plan joint action this year?
- forget your grievances and work harder than ever?
- try to work out some way in which adults will be compelled to do as much work as the young people?
- or what?

SITUATION #3   PARISH COUNCIL

Last year a record sum was raised in the Parish for the Christmas Bowl. Everyone worked very hard and it was gratifying to see such good results. However, you don't aim to rest on your laurels. You will be encouraging all groups in the Parish to get to work and see if they can't do even better this year.

SITUATION #3   COUNCIL OF ELDERS

Last year a record sum was raised in the Parish for the Christmas Bowl. Everyone worked very hard and it was gratifying to see such good results. You are pleased that the Parish Council is keen to do even better this year.

SITUATION #3   CONGREGATION

Last year a record sum was raised in the Parish for the Christmas Bowl. Everyone worked very hard and it was gratifying to see such good results. You are hoping to do even better this year.

SITUATION #4   YOUTH GROUP

You're sick of hearing young people described as "the church of tomorrow". You want your rightful place in the church of today.

Do you —

- ask for a special meeting between your group

and the Parish Council to talk through the situation?

- complain to the minister?
- stage a demonstration during the Parish Council meeting to make plain your point of view?
- carry on regardless?
- or what?

SITUATION #4　　　　PARISH COUNCIL

You have been talking recently of ways in which young people can be encouraged to take a fuller part in the life of the church. So many just come to Sunday school for a few years and that is the last you see of them. After all, young people are the church of tomorrow and mustn't be allowed just to drift away.

SITUATION #4　　　　COUNCIL OF ELDERS

You have been talking recently with the minister and the Parish Council about ways in which young people can be encouraged to stay on at Sunday school and eventually be prepared for Confirmation. After all, they are the church of tomorrow.

SITUATION #4　　　　CONGREGATION

You are always pleased to see young people in the church, even though they can be irritating at times. The important thing is that they are the church of tomorrow and for that you are willing to put up with present inconvenience.

SITUATION #5　　　　YOUTH GROUP

The kids at the Saturday night disco scrawled a lot of graffiti on the toilet walls. You found most of it and managed to scrub it off before anyone else from the church saw it. However, you missed some rather choice obscenities in one of the ladies' cubicles and some of the old women are kicking up a fuss.
Do you —

- apologise and assure everyone that it won't happen again?
- mutter about unreasonable old busybodies while you clean it off?
- leave it there and add some of your own?
- ask the Parish Council to install blackboards and chalk in the toilets?
- or what?

SITUATION #5　　　　PARISH COUNCIL

Some of the ladies of the Central Church congregation have complained about the condition of the toilets on Sunday morning after a discotheque organised by the Youth Group on Saturday night. It seems that some obscene remarks were written on the walls. While you believe it was done by outsiders, the Youth Group must bear the responsibility for anything that happens during functions they have arranged.

SITUATION #5　　　　COUNCIL OF ELDERS

On Sunday morning you heard some complaints from some of the Central Church ladies who had found obscene remarks written on the toilet walls. These seem to be the result of the Saturday night discotheque organised by the Youth Group. While you believe it was done by outsiders, the Youth Group must bear the responsibility for anything that happens during functions they have arranged.

SITUATION #5　　　　CONGREGATION

Some of the Central Church ladies are very upset at obscene remarks which they found written on the toilet walls. The young people had a dance or something on Saturday night and this filth must have been written then. It seems that the wrong kind of young person is attracted by this sort of program.

SITUATION #6　　　　YOUTH GROUP

The Parish Council has no one under thirty on it and most of the members are fifty plus. You believe the only way young people will be heard is by getting representation.

Do you —

- nominate several members of your group and vigorously campaign to get them elected?
- ask the minister for his help?
- get to know some of the people already on the Parish Council and let them know how you feel?
- give it up as a bad job and just do your own thing?
- or what?

SITUATION #6　　　　PARISH COUNCIL

As a Parish Council you take your responsibilities seriously and try to hear what the Parish is saying. Members of the Council are mostly fairly mature and have been proven leaders over the years. You are always open to ideas and suggestions from members of the congregation, but your main charter is responsibility for the overall functioning of the Parish and sectional interests must be kept in perspective.

SITUATION #6 — COUNCIL OF ELDERS

The Parish Council is a conscientious body which takes its responsibilities seriously. The membership consists largely of people over fifty, but these are the proven leaders over the years and are well fitted for their task.

SITUATION #6 — CONGREGATION

The Parish Council is a conscientious body which takes its responsibilities seriously. The membership consists largely of people over fifty who have been proven leaders over the years. Most of you are pleased to have the running of the Parish in such capable hands.

SITUATION #7 — YOUTH GROUP

You are keen to start a Christian coffee house in a back room next to the Central Church hall. You are confident that you can raise enough money and volunteer labour to get the place set up and the kids are keen to make it work.

Do you —

- ask the Parish Council for permission to go ahead?
- start looking around for some sympathetic adults to work with you on the project?
- ask the Parish Council for permission to set up the coffee house on a trial basis?
- start setting up the room?
- or what?

SITUATION #7 — PARISH COUNCIL

You have heard that some of the young people have been talking about starting a Christian coffee house on the Central Church premises. You don't want to dampen their enthusiasm, but you wonder if they realise all that is involved in such an ambitious project.

SITUATION #7 — COUNCIL OF ELDERS

Some of the young people have been talking about starting a Christian coffee house on the Central Chruch premises. They seem confident that they can handle it, but you wonder if they realise all that is involved, not only in starting it but in keeping it going, and also whether they are mature enough.

SITUATION #7 — CONGREGATION

Some of the young people have been talking about starting a Christian coffee house on the Central Church premises. You are not sure what will be the effect of having a lot of non-church young people on the property. Nor are you sure that the Youth Group will stick to what they start.

SITUATION #8 — YOUTH GROUP

After a lot of campaigning you've managed to get one of the group elected to the Parish Council. He's been to one meeting and has come away disillusioned. He complains that the members only seem interested in propping up the institutional structure. He tried to raise a question about what each organisation contributes to the spiritual life of the Parish, but no one seemed to take it seriously.

Do you —

- discuss the situation with the minister?
- encourage your member to quit going to Council meetings?
- try to work out some strategies for putting over your point of view?
- or what?

SITUATION #8 — PARISH COUNCIL

At your last meeting you welcomed newly elected members, including a young man from the Youth Group. It was a long meeting with a full agenda. The young man raised a question about the contribution of each organisation to the spiritual life of the Parish but you didn't go into it because it will be dealt with in the Annual Report. He seemed a bit impatient at how things are done, but no doubt he'll feel more at home next time.

SITUATION #8 — COUNCIL OF ELDERS

You are pleased that a member of the Youth Group has been elected to Parish Council. Since there are a lot of young people in the Parish it is good that some of them are accepting responsibility in this way. When one of the Elders spoke to this young man after his first Council meeting he seemed a little upset that "the members only seem interested in propping up the institutional structure".

SITUATION #8 — CONGREGATION

A member of the Youth Group was recently elected to the Parish Council. It is good to see young people taking responsibility in the church. So often in the past they seem to have been more interested in "knocking" it.

C_2H_5OH
ALCOHOL

A discussion game created by Brian Morgan

Purpose

C_2H_5OH (Alcohol) is a game which may be played by young people, adults, families or inter-generational groups. Its purpose is to explore through discussion the appropriateness of action in various dilemmas related to drinking alcohol.

Preparation

1. Reproduce the gameboard on a large sheet of newsprint, or several smaller sheets attached together. It should be at least 1 metre by 2 metres. Write the action paragraphs on the appropriate spots. Or copy each one on a numbered card and place it on the gameboard. Or duplicate the action paragraphs, one sheet for each team.

2. Provide a game token and a pair of dice for each team. If you have less than 12 players or want the game to last longer, use a single die.

3. Divide the group into at least four teams of not more than six people. Locate the teams conveniently around the perimeter of the room with the gameboard on the floor in the centre of the room. Since the teams are discussion groups, there needs to be sufficient space between them to minimise interference.

Playing the game

1. At the same time, every team throws the dice and moves the appropriate number of spots.

2. Each team then discusses the action paragraph from their spot for five minutes and rates it from "totally inappropriate" to "totally appropriate" on a scale of −5 to 0 to +5. "Totally inappropriate" is −5 and "totally appropriate" is +5.

3. Each team in turn reads its action paragraph, announces its rating of appropriateness, and gives the main points on which the decision was taken. Then the team moves its game token backwards or forwards according to its rating of appropriateness. (For instance, if their rating was −5, they move backwards 5 spaces.)

4. An independent recorder writes up the main points on a sheet of newsprint or a chalkboard.

5. When all teams have reported and moved, the dice are thrown again and the process continues until a team reaches the big Interrobang* mark. You could continue until all reach the Interrobang mark but it is probably better to stop when the first team reaches it.

Discussing the game

1. Talk about what winning means in this game. See if any team compromised its views in order to move forward.

2. Using the summary of main points prepared by the recorder, discuss the various dilemmas. People may wish to raise other points of view, or suggest other ways of acting.

3. Discuss the question generally. You may wish to make a list of guidelines to action.

*Interrobang is the name for a punctuation mark which combines the query (?) with an exclamation point (!), and conveys the idea of a question on which there may be several strong points of view.

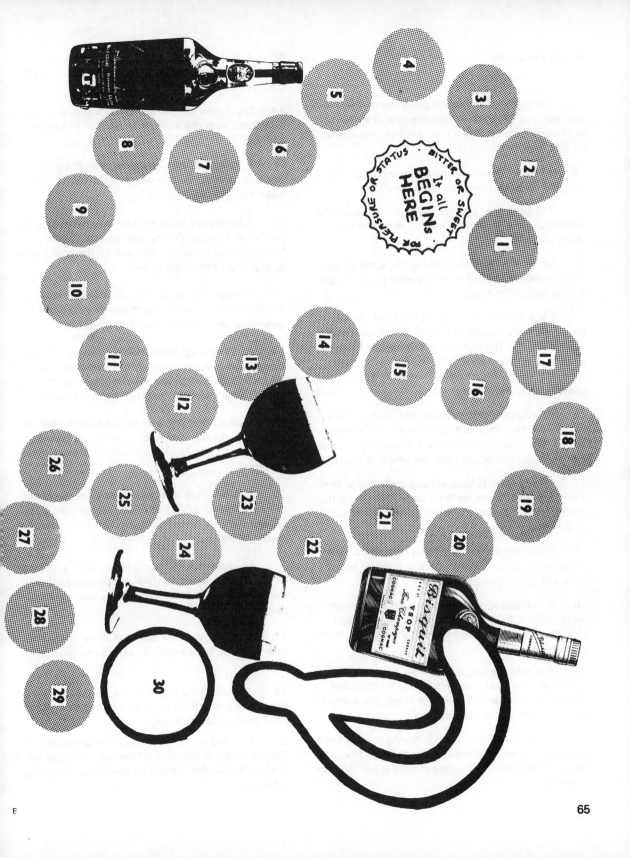

It all BEGINS HERE · BITTER OR SWEET · FOR PLEASURE OR STATUS ·

Action paragraphs

1. The leader of the youth group wants the end of year party to swing so he adds a bottle of vodka to the fruit punch. He doesn't tell anyone because he doesn't want any trouble.

2. A father frequently allows his two year old daughter to drink from his glass of beer.

3. The parents of a sixteen year old impound the alcoholic drinks her guests bring to her "sweet sixteen" party.

4. On the way to a football match, some 17 year olds decide to go to the drive-in bottle shop and get a couple dozen "tinnies".

5. For a church dinner dance the local church governing body decides that only soft drinks should be available. On the night, they arrange for a keg to be located in the garage of the member who lives next door to the church hall. Those who wish can slip over and have a drink.

6. An engaged couple decide that, despite their normal practice, they will not serve alcoholic drinks at their wedding reception on the grounds that someone might get drunk and spoil the whole celebration.

7. A father and 12 year old son are at the cricket. The son presses his father for a can of beer from the cooler. The father lets his son have one, but limits it to the one.

8. A son decides that alcohol is ruining his father's life so he empties his father's entire stock of beer, wine and spirits down the drain.

9. A husband and father never goes home from work without visiting the pub, often staying until closing. He says he needs to relax before facing home responsibilities.

10. The publican knows that the customer is drunk but since he still has money, his glass is kept filled. When the customer can no longer stand, the publican has him taken out to the footpath.

11. A matriculation student is having trouble sleeping after an evening of concentrated study. The student's mother offers a glass of port as her cure for insomnia.

12. A boy is brought home very drunk from a party. The father locks the door and refuses to allow the boy in the house.

13. Some men are going on a duck shooting trip. They take with them plenty of spirits "to keep the chill out".

14. A young woman says to her non-drinking fiance at a party, "Come on, have a drink. It will make you more interesting".

15. A family is having an interstate trip by car over the Easter holiday. On the way back on Easter Monday, they stop for lunch and all the adults have several beers before going on.

16. The young man is quite drunk but insists he can drive home. His girlfriend decides to phone her parents to get them to come and collect her.

17. At the church Drop-in Centre for young people, the manager refuses to let anyone drink alcohol on or just outside the premises. He offers to keep the drinks in the fridge until time for their owners to leave.

18. A couple are very worried and upset because both their children are involved with drug-taking. The parents begin to drink heavily to help ease their tension.

19. A father finds out that his daughter has been drinking alcohol at a friend's home after school. He requests that she stop it and join him for a pre-dinner sherry instead.

20. An unlicensed 14 year old girl, with some experience driving a truck on the farm, decides to drive her brother's car home from a party where he has passed out.

21. A mother dips the baby's dummy into rum each time the baby's colic threatens an interrupted night.

22. He goes to the pub with the boys and enjoys their company but drinks only lemon squash, despite their good-natured ribbing.

23. A young woman who has never drunk alcohol decides to drink the wine offered her at dinner rather than embarrass her hostess by asking for something different.

24.　A young student teacher whose family are non-drinkers is appointed to a regional centre where teachers regularly gather at the local hotel each Friday night. She decides to refuse the invitation to join them.

25.　A rising young executive is expected by his company to entertain clients, many of whom are heavy drinkers, for dinner. His boss tells him that on these occasions, he must be a good host and drink alcohol so the client is at ease.

26.　A young man of 18 is before the court on a first offence drunken driving charge. The judge finds him guilty and suspends his license for six months.

27.　A young man of 18 is before the court on a first offence drunken driving charge. The judge finds him guilty, but, because his work is dependent on having and driving a car, he is fined $1,000 and does not lose his license.

28.　The family of an alcoholic insist that treatment must be sought for the condition. They refuse to protect the alcoholic from public scrutiny or to lie about absenteeism.

29.　The high school headmaster arranges to run a full scale detailed education program on alcohol covering scientific, medical, social and safety factors. He makes it compulsory despite the fact that it takes time from public examination subjects.

30.　A 15 year old girl comes home from school each day to find her mother in a drunken state. The girl helps her mother keep the drinking secret from the husband and father.

the City/Country game

A game for up to 8 players of any age by Mary-Ruth Marshall

This game may be played before or during a city/country exchange, or to help city people understand the hopes and tensions of those living in the country, and vice versa.

The game was developed by Mary-Ruth Marshall with help from the Rural Strategy Committee of the Presbyterian Church in Victoria.

Preparation

1. Make the game board from the design on page

2. Make sets of T (tension) and H (hope) cards. If the game is to be played by city people, use the country cards; if it is to be played by country people, use the city cards. When playing the game with both city and country people together, shuffle the two sets of cards together and play a mixed game. Use a different colour for each set of cards.

3. Provide a counter for each player, and a pair of dice for each game.

4. Place T cards and H cards on the board.

5. Decide who will move first, and follow on.

Rules

1. All play begins from the CHURCH area in the centre of the board. Choose the exit you prefer and then move clockwise.

2. When you land on a T-square, draw a T card, read it aloud and follow its instructions. Retain any T card which says KEEP THIS TENSION CARD until you are able to cancel it through an H card or by going to a place of help. Other T cards should be set aside (those that do not say KEEP THIS TENSION CARD).

3. When you land on an H-square, draw an H card, read it aloud and follow its instructions. Turn your T cards over to indicate that they are cancelled, but keep them in front of you.

4. As soon as you have accumulated three uncancelled T cards, you MUST go to one of the five areas of help. Unless directed by a T card, you may choose the area of help you seek. When you leave the area of help, turn your T cards over to indicate that they are cancelled but keep them in front of you.

5. Throwing a double does not entitle you to a second throw.

6. The game ends when all the T cards have been read and acted upon, or at the end of a time limit (say 45 minutes). The winner is the one who has collected the fewest T cards.

7. If a situation arises for which there seems to be no rule, talk about it and decide what is fair.

8. Be sure to use the discussion questions (see below).

Discussion questions

1. How did you feel during the game?

2. What did you learn about living in the city/country?

3. Were you surprised in any way?

4. Do you know of any other tensions or hopes you would add? Look through current newspapers and magazines to get ideas for further T and H cards.

5. Choose three or four of your T cards and talk about them. How do you feel about the situation described? What might be done?

6. What will you do with your new awareness of what life is like in the city/country? What can you do to help alleviate the tensions of the city/country? Or to emphasise the hopes?

7. Was the game fair? How was it like life? How was it not like life as you know it?

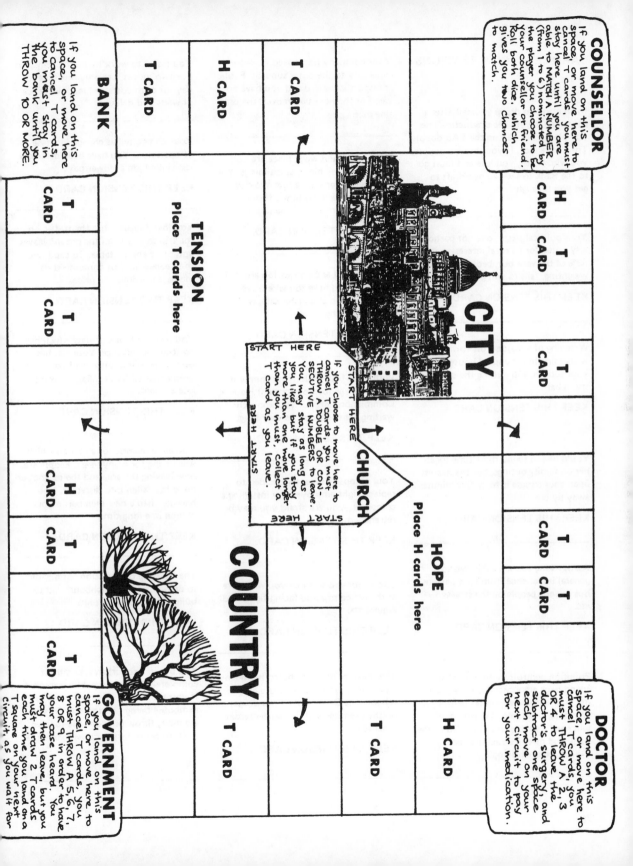

COUNSELLOR — If you land on this space, or move here to cancel T cards, you must stay here until you are able to MATCH A NUMBER (from 1 to 6) nominated by the player you choose to be your counsellor or friend. Roll both dice, which gives you two chances to match.

BANK — If you land on this space, or move here to cancel T cards, you must stay in the bank until you THROW 10 OR MORE.

TENSION — Place T cards here

CITY

CHURCH — START HERE. If you choose to move here to cancel T cards, you must THROW A DOUBLE OR CON-SECUTIVE NUMBERS to leave. You may stay as long as you like, but if you stay more than one move longer than you must, collect a T card as you leave.

START HERE

HOPE — Place H cards here

COUNTRY

GOVERNMENT — If you land on this space, or move here to cancel T cards, you must THROW A 5, 6, 7, 8 OR 9 in order to have your case heard. You may then leave, but you must draw 2 T cards each time you land on a T square on your next circuit, as you wait for

DOCTOR — If you land on this space, or move here to cancel T cards, you must THROW A 2, 3 OR 4 to leave the doctor's surgery, and subtract one space each move on your next circuit to pay for your medication.

H CARD · T CARD · T CARD · T CARD · T CARD · T CARD · H CARD · T CARD · H CARD · T CARD · T CARD · H CARD · T CARD · T CARD · T CARD

CARD SET 1: CITY TENSIONS

In an effort to prove yourself after a degrading day on the production line, you place your pay on the TAB double. Throw the dice. If you throw a double, you win. If not, you lose and must go to the Bank to seek an overdraft to get you through.

Your political party, one not particularly noted for its rural interest, wins 53% of the vote but, because of rural weighting, fails to win government.

KEEP THIS TENSION CARD.

Widening of a major cross-town artery is claiming four hundred houses in your suburb, and cutting the community in half.

KEEP THIS TENSION CARD.

You'd like to spend more time together on family outings, but the nearest open countryside is forty-five minutes away by car.

KEEP THIS TENSION CARD.

All day long you are subjected to a general impatience from sales persons, bus drivers, people on the streets, etc.

KEEP THIS TENSION CARD.

Pollution controls mean you must spend large amounts of money purifying your company's wastes before emptying them into the river. You will need a sizable overdraft. Go to the Bank and meet its qualifications TWICE before leaving.

Your company has moved from the inner-city to the outer suburbs. Public transport is limited and you have no car. For the next two moves, use only one dice.

Your home and work place are both surrounded by high-rise buildings. You see the sun for only a few mid-day hours and the wind blows furiously down the corridors of the streets.

KEEP THIS TENSION CARD.

Traffic speed and congestion are increasing. You have to make more decisions, and at a faster rate, while you are driving.

KEEP THIS TENSION CARD.

With your fifth child, your family is just too large for your present Housing Commission flat, but you know the waiting list for houses is very long.

KEEP THIS TENSION CARD.

Your company recently decided to replace eight employees by installing a computer. You are afraid you may be retrenched.

KEEP THIS TENSION CARD.

Life at home is so tense you work late at the office to avoid facing fights and arguments.

KEEP THIS TENSION CARD.

The minister of your church has been letting local youth meet there after school. The Drug Squad finds drugs on the premises and the papers sensationalise it.

KEEP THIS TENSION CARD.

You travel to work by public transport. For two moves, use only one dice to pay for both costs and inconvenience of waits and delays.

Your company has changed it style of operation. You have been offered a less-skilled job at lower pay.

KEEP THIS TENSION CARD.

You love football, but the traffic on the trip to and from the ground leaves you tense and irritable. To cap it all, the League has just announced an increase in admission prices.

KEEP THIS TENSION CARD.

You live in a block of flats which has no security entrance. Your flat has been broken into once, and you have been annoyed by drunken prowlers late at night.

KEEP THIS TENSION CARD.

You are a member of a church which was strong for many years. People are now leaving the area and the neighbourhood has fallen into disrepair. You have not had a new member in your church in a long time.

KEEP THIS TENSION CARD.

The Housing Commission has decided to demolish your neighbourhood to build cluster housing units.

KEEP THIS TENSION CARD.

You live in a suburban area almost completely lacking in public transport. If you are female, miss two turns to symbolise being tied to home. If you are male, throw only one die for two turns to cover costs of driving to work.

You travel to work by public transport. Peak hour traffic is maddening!

KEEP THIS TENSION CARD.

You go for a drive in the country and notice that there are new and expensive cars on the roads and parked on the properties. Since you drive an old, inexpensive car, you feel angry and cheated every time you hear the farmers "crying poor".

KEEP THIS TENSION CARD.

The air and water are polluted. The streets are littered.

KEEP THIS TENSION CARD.

The whole family is constantly exposed to advertising and pressures to consume. You are living beyond your income and must seek an increase of your overdraft. Go at once to the Bank.

You live in a Housing Commission building where the heat is turned off on October 1 and on again on May 1, no matter what the weather is like.

KEEP THIS TENSION CARD.

The Government announces it has cancelled plans to extend public transport to your suburb.

KEEP THIS TENSION CARD.

You have material comforts such as a house, a car and a boat, but are pushed on to achieve even more. You become increasingly anxious. Go to one of the places of help.

You bought a colour television set on hire purchase. You did not read the papers you signed and discover you are paying a very high interest rate.

KEEP THIS TENSION CARD.

Food costs are so high, you'd love to grow some of your own vegetables but have neither space nor time, and the ground is very poor.

KEEP THIS TENSION CARD.

Your job is an assembly-line one with no sense of creativity or achievement.

KEEP THIS TENSION CARD.

Your car has been broken into three times.

KEEP THIS TENSION CARD.

There are so many new people in church, you no longer feel at home there.

KEEP THIS TENSION CARD.

Noises of all kinds (traffic, power motors, diesels, televisions and stereos, motorcycles, newspaper hawkers) are becoming louder and more irritating.

KEEP THIS TENSION CARD.

Your teen-age child feels you are too dogmatic as parents, and runs away. Go at once to one of the places of help.

There are three generations in your family, all living in the same small house. Tensions abound and there are frequent arguments.

KEEP THIS TENSION CARD.

You take the children to a family film, but the cost of the film, transport and refreshments for the five of you is almost $20.

KEEP THIS TENSION CARD.

You long to receive the feeling of care and human interest, but people seem hard and insensitive.

KEEP THIS TENSION CARD AND DRAW ANOTHER AS WELL.

There are so many new people in your street, you no longer have a sense of community.

KEEP THIS TENSION CARD.

So much demolition and construction is going on, the shape of the city seems to be changing constantly. You feel a stranger in your own city.

KEEP THIS TENSION CARD.

You live on the 17th floor of a high-rise. There never seem to be more than two of the four lifts in working order. As well, they are often dirty and can be dangerous at night.

KEEP THIS TENSION CARD.

You have been involved in a chain collision in peak-hour traffic. Go to the doctor at once.

Surrounded by hundreds and thousands of people, you feel empty and lonely.

KEEP THIS TENSION CARD AND DRAW ANOTHER AS WELL.

You feel that you spend all your time rushing around, with not all that much to show for it.

KEEP THIS TENSION CARD.

Armed robbery seems to be on the increase in the city and suburbs. In addition, two cases of rape have been reported in your area in the past week.

KEEP THIS TENSION CARD.

An "adult book shop" has just opened in the local shopping centre. You wonder what the world is coming to.

KEEP THIS TENSION CARD.

All the nice little neighbourhood shops that give personal service seem to be closing down. Soon there will be nothing but supermarkets.

KEEP THIS TENSION CARD.

All week long you manage to survive by telling yourself you can relax over the weekend, but when the weekend comes you have no sense of rest or relaxation.

KEEP THIS TENSION CARD.

There are so many choices and options of things to do, you feel a strong pressure to fit everything in.

KEEP THIS TENSION CARD.

CARD SET 2: CITY HOPES

Social institutions such as clubs, churches, schools, shops and theatres are close at hand.

CANCEL ONE TENSION CARD.

Tensions and difficulties do arise, but there are many counselors and helpers.

CANCEL THREE TENSION CARDS.

Your children have paper routes and other means of earning pocket money.

CANCEL ONE TENSION CARD.

You enjoy the variety of entertainment opportunities the city offers.

CANCEL ONE TENSION CARD.

Universities and other groups provide speakers and forums covering a wide variety of interests.

CANCEL ONE TENSION CARD.

You belong to a union which works hard to see that you have a reasonable award.

CANCEL TWO TENSION CARDS.

Emergency services of all kinds are close at hand.

CANCEL TWO TENSION CARDS.

Some of the best qualified and most creative teachers choose to teach in the schools your children attend.

CANCEL TWO TENSION CARDS.

Individuals and groups are able to participate together in large joint projects (e.g. Walk Against Want).

CANCEL ONE TENSION CARD.

Your city offers a variety of ethnic restaurants and shops. Your cultural horizons are expanded.

CANCEL ONE TENSION CARD.

The school your children attend is within walking distance.

CANCEL ONE TENSION CARD.

While public transport is not perfect, it does exist and is generally reliable.

CANCEL ONE TENSION CARD.

You belong to a new, growing, vital suburban church.

CANCEL ONE TENSION CARD.

Your friends and family are, at most, a phone call away.

CANCEL ONE TENSION CARD.

Adult education courses on a wide variety of subjects are near at hand.

CANCEL ONE TENSION CARD.

Your children enjoy school excursions to a variety of places.

CANCEL ONE TENSION CARD.

Churches combine together or offer to other churches a range of special services, studies, training events, etc.

CANCEL ONE TENSION CARD.

You and your family can choose from a wide variety of clubs, sporting and hobby groups and other interests.

CANCEL ONE TENSION CARD.

Neighbourhood shops are within walking distance.

CANCEL ONE TENSION CARD.

The city stores offer a vast range of goods at competitive prices.

CANCEL ONE TENSION CARD.

CARD SET 3:
COUNTRY TENSIONS

A group of families from the city had a picnic — without your permission — on your property. They left tins, paper and food scraps littered around.

KEEP THIS TENSION CARD.

Land developers buy up most of the available acreage in your district. You can no longer afford to buy a small farm for your son.

KEEP THIS TENSION CARD.

Because of a shortage of manpower, your church is left without a minister. Stay where you are until you throw a double.

KEEP THIS TENSION CARD. YOU ARE NOT ELIGIBLE TO GO TO CHURCH UNTIL YOU CANCEL THIS CARD.

You can afford to send your children away to school, but face a moral dilemma: is it more important to support the local school or to see they get a good education in the city? Move to a place of help immediately.

The small farm next to yours has been bought by a weekend farmer. Will your relationship be good? Throw one dice. If the number is even, you get along well and may move forward. If odd, you do not move and must. . .

KEEP THIS TENSION CARD

It is almost time to harvest the wheat and you desperately need fine, warm weather. Wondering about the weather makes you tense.

KEEP THIS TENSION CARD.

You run a grocery store in a regional centre. No matter how hard you and your family work, your business success is still dependent on farmers' incomes.

KEEP THIS TENSION CARD.

The State Government decides that all river banks must be cleared of accumulated debris. This causes erosion which has eaten into a large part of your paddocks.

KEEP THIS TENSION CARD.

Every newspaper you pick up refers to rising wages and salaries in the city. But your income is now 25% less than what it was in the late 1960s.

KEEP THIS TENSION CARD.

Two city businessmen buy the neighbouring farm, clear it as a tax deduction, and then let it lie there becoming overgrown. You had hoped to buy it one day, but it is now priced out of your reach.

KEEP THIS TENSION CARD.

Your wool cheque was the lowest ever this year, and your self-esteem in the eyes of your family, your community and yourself is very low. It makes you tense, irritable and unhappy.

KEEP THIS TENSION CARD.

You live in a regional centre which has been designated a development area. There is a change of government and no one knows what the new policy will be regarding growth centres.

KEEP THIS TENSION CARD.

Your children have all had to go to the city for education and jobs. The mail service takes three days and every call is STD. You feel cut off from your children. Go at once to one of the places of help.

You have to decide what kind of farming to take up for the next five years. Decide what number you will roll with one dice. Consult the experts (other players) or trust experience (four practice throws). Move forward if you are right, backward if you are wrong.

You live in a regional centre. The cost of freight is added on to everything you buy, and you are not eligible for farm subsidies. Subtract one from every move you make from now on to pay the costs.

KEEP THIS TENSION CARD.

The Federal Government has decided that it will match dollar for dollar the cost of new farm equipment priced over $1,000. You do not have your part of the cost of a new tractor. Go to the Bank to seek an addition to your overdraft.

The Agricultural Department "experts" recommend that you switch from sheep to dairying. You do. Wool and lamb prices rise and butterfat prices fall.

KEEP THIS TENSION CARD

From the time they start school, the expectation is that your children will leave home. You lose your children at an earlier age than city parents do.

KEEP THIS TENSION CARD.

City people are purchasing more convenience and take-away foods. Your crop of pumpkins brings 40% less than last year because of reduced market.

KEEP THIS TENSION CARD.

F

You live in a regional centre whose main industry is textiles. The Federal Government lifts all textile tariffs to increase overseas earnings, and the country is flooded with cheap yard goods and clothing.

KEEP THIS TENSION CARD.

In the last ten years, almost every social institution in your small rural town has closed down: school, dance hall, shops, theatre. All that is left is the church and the pub. There is a sense of the community breaking down.

KEEP THIS TENSION CARD.

Low prices for your crop mean that the farm can no longer support you and your two sons. One of them must leave and look for a job.

KEEP THIS TENSION CARD.

Your minister is a supporter of the Labor Party while you favour the National Country Party. Ask another player to choose a number from 1 to 6. Move forward only when you can match that number with your throw of a single dice. The card is then cancelled. You cannot go to church until this happens.

A major world power withdraws from a pricing agreement and the payment for butterfat drops by a third.

KEEP THIS TENSION CARD AND DRAW ANOTHER.

You are constantly aware that decisions are made by "them" which affect you very much. You are resentful and angry.

KEEP THIS TENSION CARD.

Although you live in the country, your children have urban values, are taught by teachers with urban values, and are educated for urban living. Throw the dice and move backwards to symbolise the gap between your values and those of your children.

You live in a regional centre, although most of your friends and family live in the capital city. Your telephone account is very high because virtually every call you make must be STD.

KEEP THIS TENSION CARD.

A locust plague strips your pasture and you have to increase the feedout of hay to your stock.

KEEP THIS TENSION CARD.

The economic situation is making you very depressed and there is trouble in your marriage because of it. But marriage guidance counselors are only available in cities and provincial centres. Throw the dice. If you get 5 or under, you live close enough; 6 or over,

KEEP THIS TENSION CARD.

Your local church has been closed down and you must now go to the one in the regional centre 50 km. away.

KEEP THIS TENSION CARD. YOU ARE NOT ELIGIBLE TO GO TO CHURCH UNTIL IT IS CANCELLED.

Because you live in such a small community, your church always has young and inexperienced ministers. You do not feel that you can go to your present minister for help.

KEEP THIS TENSION CARD. YOU ARE NOT ELIGIBLE TO GO TO CHURCH UNTIL IT IS CANCELLED.

A glut on the world wheat market means overseas prices have dropped. You get less than 50% of what you had counted on.

KEEP THIS TENSION CARD.

City people think you are wealthy because of your large assets in land and stock. But there is low return on it, not much cash, and you are continually limited in what you can buy or supply for your family.

KEEP THIS TENSION CARD.

In order to live until your wheat cheque comes, you must increase your overdraft. Go to the Bank at once.

Public transport in your area has declined to a bare minimum, although many families have no private transport.

KEEP THIS TENSION CARD.

You took out a loan to pay for your property. You had a disastrous season and your wife has had to take a job just to service the loan. You feel a failure. Go at once to one of the places of help.

When you have to go to the city, it seems alien and frightful to you. You cannot wait to get away from it.

KEEP THIS TENSION CARD.

As you go about your work on the farm, you are aware that the entire community depends on you for food and sustenance, yet you are ignored by city people and the Government.

KEEP THIS TENSION CARD.

Train services between your closest station and the capital city or regional centre have been decreased and there are rumours that your station may be closed down completely.

KEEP THIS TENSION CARD.

Your grandfather settled this farm, your father lived all his life on it, and so have you. But the farm is no longer viable. What can you do? You know no other life. Go at once to one of the places of help.

A weekend farmer whose land borders yours burned off part of his property over a holiday weekend, then returned to the city. The next day a strong wind fanned the untended coals into fire and burned through two of your paddocks.

KEEP THIS TENSION CARD.

You attended agricultural college and have lots of ideas you would like to try on the farm. Your father, despite all his experience, won't go along with them. As he has control of the property and the purse strings, you must . . .

KEEP THIS TENSION CARD.

A disastrous bushfire has caused heavy stock losses throughout the district. You lost half your sheep. Go to the Government at once for aid.

"Patterson's Curse" spreads into your hill paddock, limiting its use greatly for stock.

KEEP THIS TENSION CARD.

Your son went to agricultural college and seems to have more confidence in his education than in your experience. It causes frequent disagreements in the running of the farm.

KEEP THIS TENSION CARD.

Crickets, for the third year in a row, have stripped your pastures. You need a heavy rain to seal off their eggs and prevent a fourth year of plague. Throw the dice. Eight or over, you get the rain. Under eight, no rain and . . .

KEEP THIS TENSION CARD.

Drought and lower prices have brought your income to a standstill. But you are denied unemployment benefits. Seek help at once.

City newspapers finally seem to understand some of your difficulties, but they publish letters to the editor which attack farming as inefficient and seeking favouritism. You feel powerless to defend your way of life.

KEEP THIS TENSION CARD.

CARD SET 4: COUNTRY HOPES

You share in a generosity "in kind", which is a saving to you and strengthens relationships with neighbours who are always ready to help you work your land.

CANCEL TWO TENSION CARDS.

You are virtually free of costly, tiring, time-consuming travel to and from work.

CANCEL ONE TENSION CARD.

You can make an assumption that people are honest and may be trusted.

CANCEL ONE TENSION CARD.

You have a great appreciation of nature — the seasons, cycles of nature, soil, animals, etc.

CANCEL ONE TENSION CARD.

There is a great sense of neighbourliness and community in your area. You know you can count on human resources to help you in a crisis.

CANCEL TWO TENSION CARDS.

Your church takes part in a city/country exchange with a city church. You enjoy sharing your common concerns and faith.

CANCEL TWO TENSION CARDS.

It takes only ten minutes to get to your favourite beauty spot for picnics, games, relaxation.

CANCEL ONE TENSION CARD.

The air is fresh and clean.

CANCEL TWO TENSION CARDS.

You have a good minister who loves you. He has time for you.

CANCEL ONE TENSION CARD.

The pace is slower than in the city, and you live longer.

CANCEL TWO TENSION CARDS.

During the school holidays, the whole family is available for outings and trips together.

CANCEL ONE TENSION CARD.

You join with neighbours to purchase new farm machinery together, easing the financial burden.

CANCEL ONE TENSION CARD.

You can see the results of your own work, work done with your hands, with a fair sense of immediacy.

CANCEL ONE TENSION CARD.

Regional Development plans promise to bring tertiary education facilities within daily reach for your family.

CANCEL TWO TENSION CARDS.

You can share your life with your whole family, especially your sons.

CANCEL TWO TENSION CARDS.

You do not have to lock your car.

CANCEL ONE TENSION CARD.

You are able to identify quickly with many of the Bible's parables, poems, and images.

CANCEL ONE TENSION CARD.

You can grow your own vegetables and your own chickens and eggs.

CANCEL ONE TENSION CARD.

You are your own boss.

CANCEL TWO TENSION CARDS.

There is a feeling of space, openness around you.

CANCEL TWO TENSION CARDS.

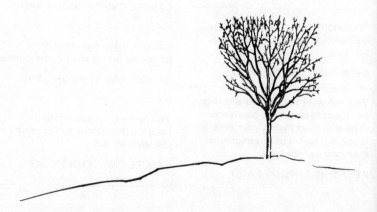

unequal RESOURCES

A game for up to 80 players, adapted by Mary-Ruth Marshall from the exercise "Unequal Resources" (1972 Annual Handbook for Group Facilitators)

Purpose

This game is designed to help players understand the feelings and actions of individuals and groups when resources are distributed unequally. It highlights behaviour when the job to be done becomes more important than the people involved, and gives an opportunity to observe the bargaining process.

You will need

1. Four copies of the Unequal Resources Task Sheet, one for each team.

Unequal Resources Task Sheet

Each team is to complete the following tasks:

1. Make a 3" by 3" square of white paper.

2. Make a 4" by 2" rectangle of red paper.

3. Make a four-link paper chain, each link in a different colour.

4. Make a T-shaped piece 3" by 5" in green and white paper.

5. Make a 4" by 4" flag, in any three colours.

The first team to complete all tasks is the winner. Bring your completed tasks to the Game Director, who will check them for accuracy.

2. Four large mailing envelopes or paper bags, each one labelled with a team's number.

3. Resources for each team:

Team 1:
1 pair scissors, 1 ruler, 10 straight pins, 3 pencils, a stapler BUT NO STAPLES, 1 quarto sheet white paper.

Team 2:
1 pair scissors, 1 bottle glue, three 5" by 5" squares of coloured paper (1 red, 1 green, 1 blue).

Team 3:
6 felt pens (one each red, green, blue, purple, orange, black) and two 5" by 5" squares of coloured paper (1 orange, 1 purple).

Team 4:
1 box staples to fit Team 1's stapler and 6 5" by 5" squares of coloured paper (2 red, 1 orange, 1 blue, 1 green, 1 purple).

DO NOT EXCEED THESE ALLOTMENTS. Other colours may be substituted, but in the same proportions. The Task Sheet must be changed if other colours are substituted.

Place each team's resources into the appropriate envelope or bag. Add a copy of the Unequal Resources Task Sheet. Seal or shut the envelope carefully so that the teams do not see one another's resources.

4. Chairs for each team. Place these as far apart as possible.

Playing the game

1. Divide the group into four teams and have them take their places.

2. Distribute the envelopes of resources, one to each team. Tell them not to open the envelopes until you give the signal.

3. Read aloud the following: "Each team has different materials and tools but each team must complete the same tasks. The tasks are listed on the Unequal Resources Task Sheet, one of which is in each envelope of resources. The first group to complete the tasks is the winner. Open your envelopes now and begin."

4. As the game goes on, observe as much group and bargaining behaviour as you can. Make notes of comments or suggestions overheard which will be useful in the debriefing session.

5. When a team declares its tasks completed and brings the items to you, check each one for conformity to standards. Reject any which are not precisely the size requested. Teams which fail to meet standards may return to work.

6. Declare as winner the first team to complete all five tasks exactly as described.

Debriefing (use these questions first to help people express their emotions)

1. What happened in the game?

2. How did you feel about your team's resources?

3. How did you feel about the other teams' resources?

4. Was there violence or conflict?

5. Between which teams was there conflict and how did it start?

6. How was the conflict resolved?

7. What helpful offers or bargains were made?

8. Who took the initiative in planning strategy?

9. Was there any individual or team you did not trust? Why?

10. Did anyone feel ignored or treated with lack of consideration?

11. In the game, did you do anything contrary to your own values? How did you feel about this?

Discussion (use these questions after everyone has had a chance to talk about feelings and experiences)

1. What were the factors which helped the winning team to win?

2. What were the factors which helped the losing team to lose?

3. How was this game like life? How was it unlike life?

4. What nations are like Team 1? Team 2? Team 3? Team 4?

5. Which team is your nation most like? Why?

6. What groups in your society are like Team 1? Team 2? Team 3? Team 4?

7. What did you learn about conflict in this game?

8. How can you apply those learnings to life?

9. What did you learn about power in this game?

10. How can you apply those learnings to life?

11. Which behaviour in the game could be described as in keeping with the teachings of Jesus? Which could be described as inconsistent with the teachings of Jesus?

Adapting the game

You can alter the complexity of tasks and distribution of resources to fit many different groups and age levels. Children can play this game, and it is very appropriate for intergenerational or cross-age groups. Do not increase the amount of material distributed unless you also increase the tasks. It is the need for resources which provides the basic interaction of the game.

BREAK DOWN THE WALLS...

A game by Pat Baker for four players

This is a game about the walls that divide people and nations. It starts with the players isolated, each cut off from the others by dividing walls. The aim of the game is first to break down the dividing walls and then to come together outside the walled area.

The game is played by four people, and is co-operative rather than competitive. An element of competition is added when two or more groups of four play simultaneously on different boards. Then the competition is between the groups, to see which is united first.

You will need

- A game board (see page 80).
- A set of "hope" cards (see page 82).
- A coloured counter for each player.
- A single die.
- Some means of making removable walls, e.g., a soft black pencil or plasticene.

The board

- The playing board is divided into four separate areas. The "walls" are marked by heavy rules in the diagram on page 80.

- Since the position of the walls will change during the course of the game, you will need to mark them in some additional way. You may —

  (a) shade the walls with a soft black pencil, like this ▦▦▦ and use a rubber to remove the, or
  (b) build plasticene walls, and break them when necessary.

Note: One very effective way of playing this game if you have the room to do it is to mark a huge game board on the floor with chalk and let the players be their own counters. The walls can be marked with a different colour, or you can make walls of chairs,

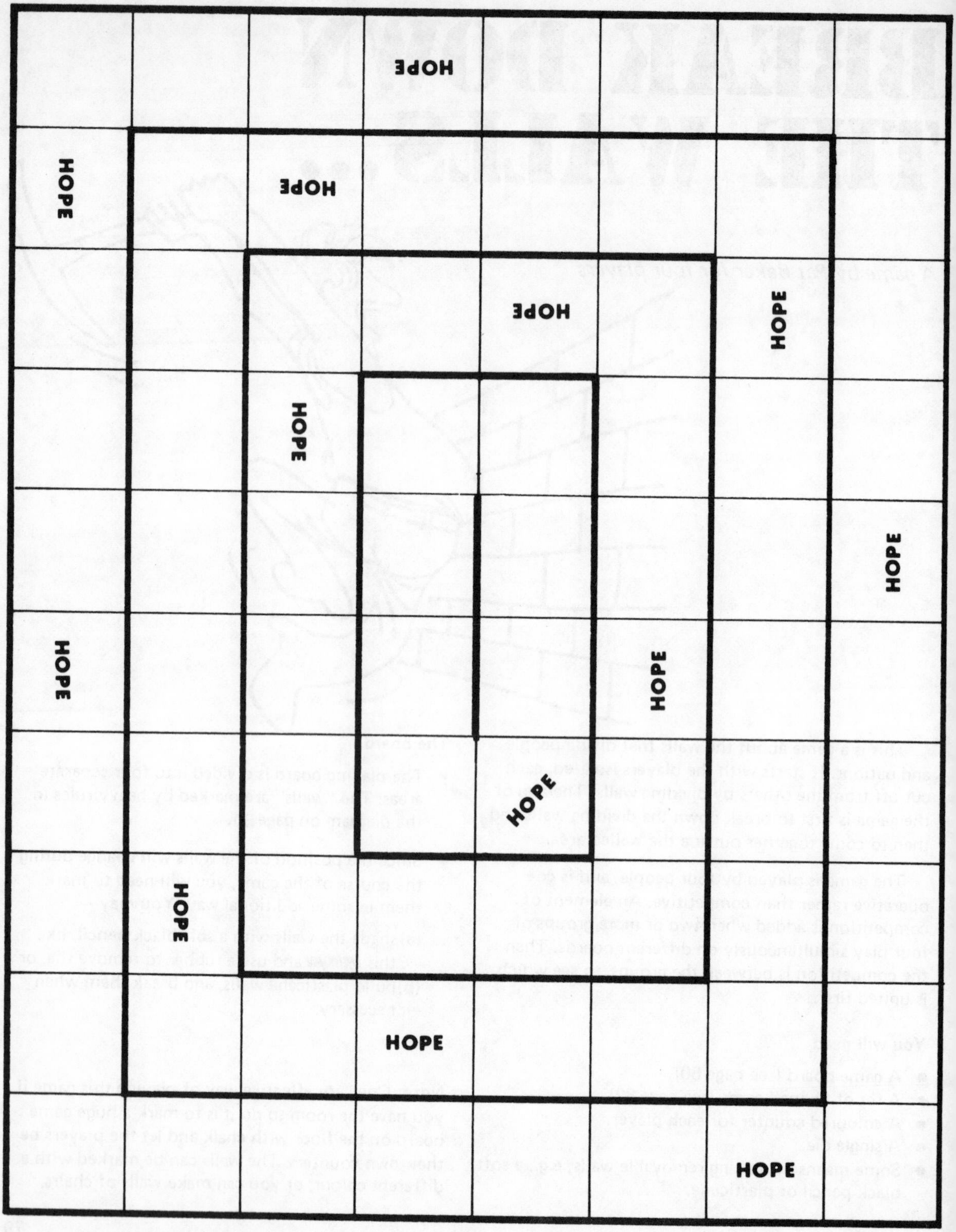
HOPE
HOPE
HOPE
HOPE
HOPE
HOPE
HOPE
HOPE
HOPE
HOPE
HOPE
HOPE
HOPE

books, rolled-up newspapers, whatever is available. If you play on a giant board you may also like to make a giant die out of a carton.

The hope cards

● There are 24 hope cards —

10 describing conditions which divide people and nations, and offer little hope,

10 describing conditions which break down barriers, and are real signs of hope,

and 4 marked "no change".

Preparing to play

1. Set up the walls for the beginning of the game.

2. Shuffle the hope cards and place them face down beside the board.

3. Each choose a playing area and a counter. Only one player is allowed in each enclosed area.

4. Place your counter on any hope square within your area.

To play

1. The player in the innermost area begins, by throwing the die. When you throw 1, 2, 3, 4, or 5, you move that number of squares, in whichever direction you choose (as long as you do not cross any walls or reverse your direction in the middle of a turn).

2. Should you throw a 6 you do not move, but you do pick up the top hope card. (You also pick up a hope card when you land on a hope square.)

3. When you draw a hope card, read it aloud, and take the appropriate action:

A "break" card allows you to break down a section of the wall adjacent to the square where your counter is.

A "wall" card compels you to fence in one side of your square.

A "no change" card means you do nothing.

4. Place the used hope cards face up in a separate pile. When the cards are all used up, reshuffle them and place them face down again.

5. As walls are broken down, players may move freely through the gaps.

6. Your aim is for all four players to break out into the open area beyond the walls. However, no one may move outside (even if the outer wall is broken) until it is possible for everyone to get out (i.e. until there are gaps in all the inner walls).

7. You may not pass or jump over another player's counter, nor may you land your counter on a square already occupied by another player. If you **do** collide with another player, you must both return your counters to the innermost area of the board.

8. Should you become trapped in a square surrounded by walls on all sides, you may not move, but you may continue to throw the die in the hope of throwing a 6 and perhaps drawing a card which will enable you to break down one of the walls. (Or you may hope that another player will break down the wall to free you.)

9. Should new walls cut any player off from the others after some have already moved outside the walled area, those who have moved outside must return to the innermost area.

10. Remember that the idea of the game is not to be the first outside the walls, but to get everyone outside in the shortest possible time.

Some questions for afterwards

1. What were you, personally, trying to do during the game?

2. How did you feel about the walls?

3. How did you help one another? Did you do as much as you could have done?

4. Did you ever collide with another player and have to go back to the centre of the board? How did you feel about that?

5. Did you ever sacrifice your own advantage to help someone else?

6. What did you learn about the walls that divide people and nations?

Hope cards

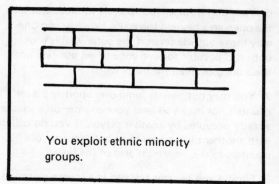

You exploit ethnic minority groups.

Draw a broken wall (as above) on all the cards below.

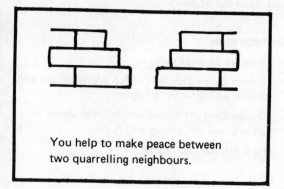

You help to make peace between two quarrelling neighbours.

Draw an unbroken wall (as above) on all the cards below.

Your natural resources are in the control of multi-national corporations.

You have a closed immigration policy.

You arm for war.

You cut off diplomatic relations with your neighbours.

You fear invasion by a foreign power.

You are testing nuclear weapons.

You don't speak the same language as your neighbours.

You want to be in a position of power.

Your fishing boats are arrested inside your neighbours territorial waters.

NO CHANGE

NO CHANGE

NO CHANGE

NO CHANGE

You and your neighbours sign a treaty of peace and friendship.

You hold democratic elections for the first time in 20 years.

There is equal opportunity for all in your multi-racial society.

You and your neighbours agree on trade policy.

You set up a student exchange scheme with other countries.

You provide technical aid to developing countries.

You begin a cultural exchange with other countries.

You send immediate aid when a neighbouring country is hit by an earthquake.

You share food surpluses with neighbouring countries.

zinga

By Pat Baker

"Zinga" is a simulation game designed to help people experiment with and examine various attitudes to world needs and overseas aid. It is a role-playing game, but with group rather than individual roles. The game is designed for youth groups, but is suitable for adults.

Number of players

Role descriptions are provided for eight different groups. This may be more than you can handle. Each group needs at least two members, preferably more to give a reasonable interchange of ideas. If you don't have enough people for eight groups, start with the Zingan delegation and add as many other groups as you can manage. A total of eight people (four groups of two) would be the minimum number with which you could hope to have a satisfactory simulation.

Time

The ratio of time needed for Preparation: Presentation : Evaluation is roughly 1 : 1 : 1 for younger youth. Older youth and adults might be expected to need more time for Evaluation. One hour is the minimum time that should be allowed for the total experience.

Resources

Enough copies of the situation sheets and data sheets for each group to have one. A role description for each group. In addition you will need to provide material for the group activities 4 and 5 as set out on the situation sheet (cardboard, newsprint, scissors, paste, felt pens, coloured paper, assorted odds and ends).

Procedure notes for the leader

Divide the players into groups. It is more important to seek a balance of ability than of numbers. Set the scene for the game by reading aloud the first two paragraphs on the situation sheet.

Give each group a situation sheet, a data sheet, and a role description. Indicate the other resources available and allot or allow each group to choose a suitable meeting place for the Preparation phase. Arrange for a warning to be given 5 minutes before the Preparation time is due to end, and for a signal to summon the delegations to the Congress. Answer questions for clarification.

Preparation

The groups move to their meeting places and work on their appointed tasks.

Presentation

Summon the delegates to the Congress. The "President of Zinga" takes the chair. This role may be taken by a leader or, when the simulation is used with an adult group, the Zingan delegation may be asked to elect a President during the Preparation period. The President welcomes the delegations and invites them, in turn, to identify themselves and bring greetings. After the greetings the President invites statements on world needs and proposals for meeting them. Depending on how much time is available, interjections and debate may be encouraged.

Evaluation

Bring the presentation to an end and ask the participants to derole. (Have them remove all signs of group identity and mix up so that they are no longer sitting in groups.) Discuss the game by looking at these questions:

- How did you feel about the game? What was good? What bugged you?

- How did you feel about your group's position? What were its strengths? Its weaknesses? What do other groups see as the strengths and weaknesses of this group's point of view?

- Did you feel that you had allies in any of the other groups? Were any of them your enemies?

- What was the best proposal made for meeting world needs?

SITUATION SHEET

Next year has been proclaimed International Progress Year. To mark the beginning of the year there will be a World Progress Congress in Zinga, a developing country which has recently gained its independence. The Congress will begin on Christmas Eve this year and end on January 1.

Among the delegates attending the Congress will be representatives of various groups from Australia and New Zealand. The people of Zinga will also be represented. A major focus of the Congress will be the differences between rich and poor nations and what can be done about them.

In preparation for the World Progress Congress, each group of delegates must complete the following tasks:

1. Develop a clear and concise statement of their attitudes to world needs and to aid programs.

2. Develop a proposal setting out what they think is the best way to solve world problems such as hunger, over-population, and the great differences between rich and poor countries.

3. Appoint a spokesperson to present their views at the Congress.

4. Prepare a Christmas greeting and/or gift for the people of Zinga.

5. Develop a symbol, badge, uniform, song, salute, or other expression of their group identity — that is, something which shows who they are and what they stand for.

DATA SHEET: Zinga

Zinga is a developing country. It comprises three major islands and an unknown number of smaller islands covering a total area of around 70,000 square kilometres. The population is 13,000,000.

The economy is largely rural, though there is a struggling textile industry and the government is working at developing other industries such as canning (fish and tropical fruit products). The considerable rubber plantations are all foreign owned, but the government is rumoured to be considering nationalisation of these. In the early colonial days, tin was mined, but the deposits were worked out years ago. Several multi-national companies were engaged in mineral exploration at the time of independence. Their operations were suspended and the government has made it quite clear that if there are minerals to be found it will be Zingans who find them and the Zingan economy which profits.

The majority religion of Zinga is Buddhism (70% of the population), with about 20% Moslems and 10% Christians.

ROLE DESCRIPTIONS (one to each group)

Zingans

You represent the people of the host country at the World Progress Congress. Many of the other delegates will be from wealthier nations. While you don't want to beg, you hope they will come to recognise the needs of poorer countries and will go back to their own countries with ideas of the kind of help that will be most valuable. Developing countries don't want charity. They do want fair dealing — and the kind of aid that will help them to help themselves, with dignity.

You understand that some of the delegations will be bringing Christmas greetings. Christmas does not have any special significance in Zinga, except to the minority group of Christians. There are no Christians in your delegation.

You must remember that you are acting as hosts to this Congress. You must try to remain polite at all times.

Isolationists

You believe that "charity begins at home". There are needy people in your own country; you think you should be helping them rather than people far away with strange cultures and customs. Therefore you are against giving aid to developing countries, even though you feel very sorry for people who haven't enough to eat or who can't get jobs. You think their government ought to be doing something about it.

Self helpers

You believe people get what they deserve. If people in some parts of the world haven't enough it's because they're a lot of lazy bludgers who think the rest of the world owes them a living. People and nations have to work for what they want. That's why your own country has a high standard of living; energy and intelligence have got you where you are today! You admit that some countries may need a bit of help to get them started, but they have to show that they deserve it. And there must be strict control of any aid that **is** given to make sure that it is not misused.

Project pushers

You are very much committed to sharing what you have with those who are in need. You believe that one of the most effective ways is by support of limited long-term projects (e.g., training schemes, programs to improve food yields and harness scarce resources). You accept that any aid given is just a drop in the bucket, but you maintain that enough drops can actually fill a bucket.

Delicate balancers

You don't like thinking about world problems because everything is so complicated. For example, when health care is improved in African or Asian countries it just makes the hunger problem worse because there are more people to be fed. Or you try to improve farm production by providing machinery or more efficient tools and you throw a whole lot of people out of work. Then the out-of-work peasants flock to the cities and create a further problem with slums. Whatever you do seems to cause more problems than it solves. Maybe it's better to do nothing at all.

Simple lifestylers

You are very concerned about all aspects of world need. You believe that people in your country are too greedy, always wanting more of everything and using up more than their share of the world's resources. You believe that if people could be convinced to live more simply it would be a start towards solving the world's problems. A more simple lifestyle would mean that your country would have more to give away to those in need, too.

Little people

You acknowledge that you are only the little people. You have no power to do anything about world problems. Governments are the only ones with sufficient power to do anything significant. Ordinary little people and church and charitable organisations can't really hope to make any impression on the problems. If you want anything to happen, you have to persuade the government to act, giving aid to developing countries and, particularly, ensuring that its trade policies are fair to poor countries with a limited range of products to sell. If you can't move the government, the game is lost.

Zingan Student's Association

You represent Zingan students who have been studying in Australia and New Zealand. Coming from a poor country like Zinga, you have been amazed at the comparative wealth of your hosts. They don't seem to know when they are well off. From the news media you have learned that the people there are not satisifed with their standard of living and want to raise it even higher. Yet people on welfare are wealthy by Zingan standards. Despite the personal kindness of most of the people you have met there, you sense a basic selfishness and a lack of sensitivity to wider needs.

One member of your delegation is a Christian.

MIND FLINTS

— some ideas that could be developed into games

After playing other people's games for a while, many of us decide that we would like to try making up our own games. Here are a few ideas you might like to play around with.

TOWN PLAN

Plan a town, including residential, industrial, commercial and recreational areas. You might start with a map — either a survey map of an actual area or a home-made map of an imaginary one. If you make your own, it would be a good idea to use graph paper. Show land elevation, and maybe include a stream or some sea coast. Indicate the direction of the major city and any other important factors. The task for the players is to plan a town for that area. If you want to involve a lot of players you could have them meet in groups representing sectional interests (e.g., Chamber of Commerce, sports association, Council of Churches, etc.) to talk about their needs and ideas and then send delegates to a planning meeting. You could have everyone as spectators at the planning meeting, with the power to replace their delegate if he/she is not doing the job to their satisfaction.

BUDGET

A mission board, a local church administration, a youth club board of management, or a sports association budgets for the coming year. (You may be able to work with actual figures from a past year's income and expenditure.) Plan how to handle a short fall or what to do with a windfall, or maybe both. You could perhaps start with an expected serious deficit and, after the group has grappled with the problem of cutting expenditure, feed in a message that a wealthy benefactor has presented you with a sum far in excess of the deficit.

FREEWAY

Participants are members of a special commission appointed to assess plans for building a freeway to by-pass the congested central area of a real or imaginary city. Start with a map on which the proposed route is marked. At least some members of the commission could have a special interest in the freeway, either because their houses will be demolished, or because it will affect their business one way or another, or because it will make it harder for them to get to church, or whatever reasons you like to introduce. The commission should have the power to suggest an alternative route for the freeway or even to veto the proposal altogether.

LEISURE PARK

The community has received a bequest of land (money too, if you like), with the proviso that it be used to provide recreational facilities for the residents in the form of a leisure park. Plan the best way of using the bequest. Participants could play themselves, or you could assign roles that would ensure that many interests were introduced.

COMMUNICATION GAME

Have two or more teams with a simple message to communicate to each other, but not speaking the same language. You might like to ensure confusion and conflict by giving each group a different basic vocabulary of words and/or gestures to express such things as friendship, anger, pleasure, "yes" and "no" (making sure that some are direct opposites). Or let the teams make up their own language.

CHOOSING A LEADER

Participants are members of a group responsible for choosing a leader (of a political party, a head prefect, a team captain, a company president). Make up a "dossier" on each candidate, containing all the information the electors would need to have to make a responsible choice. (The candidates should be fictional rather than actual persons.) Circulate the dossiers and ask the electors to make a choice, preferably by consensus. Discussion afterwards can deal with the qualities we look for in our leaders.